Because of This I Rejoice

BECAUSE
of This I
REJOICE

Reading Philippians During Lent

MAX O. VINCENT

UPPER
ROOM BOOKS®
NASHVILLE

Cover design: Lindy Martin, Faceout Studio
Cover image: Shutterstock Images
Interior design and typesetting: PerfecType | Nashville, TN

Library of Congress Cataloging-in-Publication Data

Names: Vincent, Max O., author.
Title: Because of this I rejoice : reading Philippians during Lent / Max O. Vincent.
Description: Nashville : Upper Room Books, 2018. | Includes bibliographical references.
Identifiers: LCCN 2018026824| ISBN 9780835817936 (print) | ISBN 9780835817943 (mobi) | ISBN 9780835817950 (epub)
Subjects: LCSH: Bible. Philippians—Devotional literature. | Lent. | Devotional literature.
Classification: LCC BS2705.54 .V56 2018 | DDC 227/.606—dc23
LC record available at https://lccn.loc.gov/2018026824

for

KEV and MIV

I thank my God every time I remember you.
—Philippians 1:3

CONTENTS

ACKNOWLEDGMENTS

I want to begin by saying thanks to Upper Room Books for considering publication of this material. Joanna Bradley, Acquisitions Editor, graciously guided this project from the beginning. Erin Palmer had the more difficult task of delivering me from my love of the passive voice and nominalization. The staff at Upper Room Books are encouraging and supportive of their authors. I cannot imagine writing this book with any other group.

I wrote this manuscript while serving as pastor of Inman Park UMC. The congregation provided a joyful place to serve together in ministry. Comments in the text about my congregation refer to Inman Park. During the editing of the text, I became pastor of St. James UMC in Atlanta, Georgia. St. James has welcomed our family with the type of joyful hospitality Paul calls for in Philippians.

I have more friends than I can name who have endured conversations where Paul and the Philippians were uninvited guests. To those who not only tolerated my verbal presentations of Paul but also were willing to read selections of this material, I owe a double debt.

Without my wife, Kristen, and my son, Matthew, I would not have found the time, the energy, or the will to work through this material. They provide the context of joyful Christian living that made me think I first understood something of what Paul was writing in his little letter. I dedicate the book to them because they make me a better Christian (but the defects are all my own doing).

Introduction: Laughing on Ash Wednesday

We associate Lent with confession, so I confess I like Lent. I look forward to Ash Wednesday. I love the lights and carols at Christmas, the crowds and music of Easter. I enjoy the enthusiasm of Pentecost, celebrating the arrival of the Spirit with color and energy. Even as a child, I awaited the end of summer and the beginning of fall when church attendance would increase as families returned from vacations. But each year I find myself growing in anticipation of beginning Lent with worship on Ash Wednesday.

Lent, the season of forty days preceding Easter, reminds us of the time Jesus spent in the wilderness, fasting and facing temptation. During this season, we devote ourselves to acts of piety and abstinence in remembrance of the discipline and fasting Jesus lived in the desert. Since Sunday is a feast day, we do not count Sundays in the forty days of

Lent. Counting back forty days from Easter, skipping Sundays, the fortieth day is a Wednesday. We call this day that starts the season of Lent *Ash Wednesday*.

In Ash Wednesday worship services, we commit to fasting and discipline during Lent. We promise more time for such disciplines as prayer, scripture reading, and giving. We may see the time we devote to additional spiritual disciplines as our Lenten fast, or we may promise to abstain from particular activities or substances. We admit our failure to keep promises like this in the past. We confess.

Ashes mark worshipers with a sign of a cross, reminding us that our failures are part of our frail human nature, prone to decay. These ashes come from palm fronds saved from the previous Palm Sunday service. After nearly a year, we burn these instruments of praise to remind us that we too shall return to dust. This act of imposing ashes on worshipers gives the day its name.

When I was younger, I thought Ash Wednesday depressing. The crowds are small, much smaller than Christmas and Easter. Worshipers are not as enthusiastic on Ash Wednesday as on Pentecost. The music, if there is music, is melancholy.

Now I look forward to Ash Wednesday worship. I joyfully recommit to life as a disciplined follower of Jesus. I accept God's forgiveness of my inability to keep promises I have made in the past. I realize that, apart from God's grace, my efforts are as fleeting as ashes formed from decaying palm branches. I give thanks for the work of God's grace despite my human nature as someone marks my forehead with ashes and utters, "Remember you are dust and to dust you shall return."

I do not sit and ponder death most waking moments, but something about remembering mortality enables us to enjoy life, to live life as a thankful response to God's giving us the opportunity to be here in this time and place. I enjoy Ash Wednesday's invitation to live in greater awareness of God's grace at work in our lives and the world.

To put it another way, on Ash Wednesday we consider the purpose of our life in light of what we often call the end of life. The Westminster Shorter Catechism says our purpose is to worship God and enjoy God forever. Lenten disciplines make us more conscious of giving glory to God and enjoying God's presence in our life. However, Lent in general and Ash Wednesday in particular often seem devoid of joy.

Denying Self, Acknowledging God

During Lent, we talk of self-examination and "giving up something." To those who are unfamiliar with these practices, Lent may sound like a Christian self-improvement season. We focus on bad things we need to eliminate from our lives. We replace our normal greeting, "The Peace of Christ be with you," with the Lenten alternative, "So what are you giving up this year?" We confess and examine our lives. We talk about our struggles, the times we fail to keep our Lenten disciplines. Lent may seem composed of difficult tasks we endure to get to Easter, dues paid to attend the sunrise service.

Do we focus on ourselves too much in Lent? Have we lost sight of how our Lenten practices are meant to draw us closer to God? Is our lack of focus on God depriving us of Lenten joy?

Disciplines like giving extra time to prayer, reading the Bible, giving to others, and other devotional exercises help us to be more aware of God's presence. Time given up to these activities should be joyful experiences of God's grace working in and through us. Fasting is not about proving our love to God but about ridding ourselves of loves that compete with or stifle our awareness of God's love and claim for us.

When I share with others my joy in Lent, I receive one of several similar reactions. The most common response conveys fear that I may be an introspective masochist for enjoying Lent. My congregants and colleagues say it more politely, but their comments betray their thoughts. While we were planning Ash Wednesday worship and I shared my enjoyment of Lent, one of my friends responded: "You like Lent! Are you mad? Who could enjoy all those prayers of confession, the extra discipline, and self-denial? Are you sure you know what Lent is?" Another common response goes something like this: "You are joking, right? We take Lent seriously. It's not fun and games, certainly not something about which you should be joking. I cannot think of a more solemn occasion than Lent, especially Ash Wednesday."

These responses make me wonder, *Is Lent meant to be depressing? Are spiritual disciplines supposed to sound like the drudgery of chores? Is confession nothing more than taking out our spiritual trash, praying akin to writing out the grocery list? Am I wrong to look forward to Ash Wednesday? Am I sacrilegious in finding joy in Lent?*

To make matters worse, I find it difficult not to laugh on Ash Wednesday at the time and place we identify as the high point of the liturgy for the day.

Let me set the scene for you: I am a pastor. For important days in the church, I am expected to be present and at the center of the action. I perform weddings and funerals, preside at Communion and baptisms. Though I do not preach every Sunday of the year, I am expected to preach on days like Easter and Christmas. So, on Ash Wednesday, people look for me to be at the center of the activity. Imposing ashes and saying, "Remember you are dust, and to dust you shall return," is the central act of worship for Ash Wednesday. This act names the day. So, as the pastor, I'm expected to be involved in this activity. I may not be the one who places the ashes on those worshiping, but I am supposed to bless and oversee the distribution of the ashes.

I do think this moment is serious. To stand before someone, place ashes on his or her forehead, and say "Remember your mortality" is no light matter. To ask people to consider our dust-like nature is serious business. However, I want to laugh in this moment. I am not flippant or lighthearted. I believe the liturgy invites us to laugh at this point.

Shortly before this moment of imparting the ashes, I read the Gospel text for the day. In our church and in most Christian churches, this reading comes from the Sermon on the Mount, Matthew 6:1-21. Just moments before I stand to put ashes on the foreheads of people, I read these words of Jesus, "Beware of practicing your piety before others. . . . And whenever you fast, do not look dismal, like the hypocrites, for they disfigure their faces so as to show others that they are fasting" (Matt. 6:1, 16). Within minutes of reading these words, I stand at the altar rail, ashes in hand, and encourage worshipers to come forward and let me disfigure their foreheads.

Surely I am not the only one who finds the irony of our ritual funny.

Is joy out of place in a season of self-denial and spiritual devotion? The ushers would likely escort me out of our church if I started laughing at this point in the service. But perhaps the liturgy invites us to focus less on what we do or do not do, less on what we deny or add during Lent. What if Ash Wednesday encourages us to grow joyfully in our acknowledgment of God through spiritual disciplines? What if we are meant to hold ourselves as lightly as the dust from last year's palm fronds?

Paul, the Cross, and Joy

One year, given my growing confusion about joy in Lent, I committed to reading the book of Philippians as one of my Lenten disciplines. I chose this letter because many scholars consider Paul's teaching on the cross vital to interpreting Philippians. I thought focusing more on the cross would rid me of my suspect Lenten joy.

If you know Philippians, you also know Paul uses the word *joy* more in this letter than in any other. Gary Bloomquist argues that joy permeates every section of this letter; it is part of what holds together the letter.[1] Paul shares in Philippians how he practices certain disciplines with great joy. It characterizes his devotional practices. Focusing less on ourselves and more on how these practices connect us to Christ imbues the activities with joy.

Through the resurrection, God transforms the cross from a symbol of shame to a source of Christian living. Joy for Christian living flows from the cross. The cross moves us to focus on God instead of self and to conform our bodies to the life of Christ. Spiritual practices like prayer, witnessing, and giving are joyful acts for us as we live gospel-shaped lives. Reading this letter, in which the cross is so central and joy so prominent, I became convinced that God invites us all to a joyful transformation though disciplines that mold our lives to the life of Christ.

This book is a Lenten study of Philippians. What follows is a series of meditations on Paul's teaching about joyfully practicing spiritual disciplines. I do not cover all spiritual disciplines or all the nuances of each passage. This study is not a commentary on Philippians. The resource list at the end of the book includes commentaries that I found helpful in my reading. The meditations encourage you to adopt some of the same joyful practices that mark Paul's life.

Likewise, I do not offer this study as a "How to Be More Joyful" guide as if Paul says pray more, give more, deny yourself more, and you will find joy. Paul practices these devotional acts joyfully rather than hoping they will bring joy. Something at the heart of Christian living makes these disciplines not drudgery but rather joyful expressions of the life of faith. That *something* is the gospel, which transforms even the cross into a symbol of triumph. This same gospel conforms us to the life of Christ. Because of this, we too rejoice.

The six chapters coincide with the six weeks in Lent. A passage from Philippians structures each chapter. You could read the assigned passage from Philippians and the chapter on Sunday. At the end of the chapter, I have listed a selection of scripture passages related to the material we have covered: one passage for each remaining day of the week. Each day, you might read the passage several times. On the first reading, consider how the passage relates to Philippians. Read it again as you contemplate what the passage tells you about how you practice this discipline in your life. You might want to keep a journal of your thoughts and insights from each passage. Finally, read the passage again as a closing act of worship. After the scripture readings, I have posed questions for you to consider as you contemplate and interact with the material. You might use these questions for personal reflection at the end of the week or to guide discussion in a group study. I have provided a Leader's Guide at the end of the book for those who may be using this material in a small-group format.

Since Lent begins on Ash Wednesday, I have included some scripture passages and questions at the end of this introduction to help you start your Lenten journey. I pray that this Lent will be a joyful season of drawing closer to God and that you too will have the faith to face whatever lies ahead with the confidence Paul expresses when he says, "No matter what, because the gospel is furthered, I will rejoice" (1:18, AP).

DAILY SCRIPTURE READINGS

Matthew 6:1-21   Matthew 3:13–4:11
Mark 1:9-13   Luke 3:21-22; 4:1-13

QUESTIONS FOR REFLECTION

1) What do you think of first when you hear the word *Lent*?

2) How have you observed Lent in the past? Have you participated in any focused studies or adopted new spiritual disciplines? How did these practices make you feel?

3) When you hear Paul's name, what comes to mind? How can you think of Paul as a joyful Christian?

4) What do you hope to get out of this study?

Week One: Joyful Prayer

Philippians 1:1-11

"Constantly praying with joy in every one of
my prayers for all of you."
—Philippians 1:4

I don't know when, but at some point in my past, prayer became a chore. My earliest memories of prayer involve my parents kneeling with me beside my bed, teaching me prayers like "Now I lay me down to sleep" and The Lord's Prayer before I climbed into bed and fell asleep. These are pleasant, fond memories, so I do not think praying seemed like a chore then.

My next memories of prayer also involve going to sleep at night. At this stage, my parents did not accompany me. I was old enough to prepare myself for bed. Before going to my room, I would find my parents and tell them good night. Often they sent me to bed with reminders to wash my face, brush my teeth, and say my prayers. I think this is when I began to view saying prayers as a chore, just one item on a checklist to complete before climbing under the covers.

I knew not washing my face would leave me dirty and could cause my face to breakout. My mother and my doctor, who had taken lots of time to explain this issue to me, would be disappointed if I did not wash my face. I knew not brushing my teeth could cause cavities. My dentist would be disappointed, and my father would be unhappy with the increased bill at the dentist's office. So what would happen if I did not pray? Would God be disappointed? Would God tell my parents? (Yes, I was more afraid of my parents learning about my negligence than God. I had discovered God was quicker to forgive and to forget than my parents.) This problem was too complex for a tired little boy to solve. So, I washed my face, brushed my teeth, and said my prayers. Most nights I tried to do all three anyway. (Please do not tell my parents.) Some nights I did not pray. Other nights,

I prayed but with all the enthusiasm of someone taking out the trash for the third time in the same week.

As I got older, this bedtime prayer attitude filtered into other times of prayer: prayer before meals, prayer in worship, prayer during my morning devotional reading. I did not stop praying. I did not think prayer a waste of time or unimportant. I merely viewed prayer as something that had to be done, like cutting the grass or cleaning the house. Prayer was routine, a duty. I missed any sense of joy in prayer.

Then I found Paul's prayer at the beginning of Philippians. Most of Paul's letters begin with a prayer or at least a report of prayer for the congregation addressed. This prayer report is part of Paul's routine, a discipline of Paul's writing style. We expect it in his correspondence. Paul thanks God that people all around the world talk about the faith of the Romans. (See Romans 1:8.) He thanks God that the Corinthians receive grace. (See 1 Corinthians 1:4.) He gives thanks for the hope and steadfastness of the Thessalonians. (See 1 Thessalonians 1:3.) Only in his letter to the Galatians does Paul drop this habit of reporting on his prayers of thanksgiving for the congregation. Paul's expression of constant joy in his prayer for the Philippians strikes me (1:4). I wonder how Paul kept his routine of praying for his congregations from becoming a burden. How, amid the practice of disciplined prayer, did Paul maintain a sense of joy? What is the source of joy in his prayers for these Philippians?

Seeing One Another in Christ

I first thought that perhaps Paul prays for the Philippians so joyfully because they were terrific people. Paul writes in part to thank them for supporting his ministry with financial gifts (4:18). Giving thanks for gifts has never bored me. Maybe Paul was happy about their financial support. Perhaps the Philippians are better Christians than the ones Paul encountered in Corinth or Thessalonica.

The further I read in the letter, the more I realized that Paul does not say the Philippians are perfect or even better than other Christians. He prays that they continue to grow and mature in Christ. He realizes they suffer from human limitations and are as prone to arguments, divisions, and disagreements (4:2-3) as members of any other congregation. The roots of Paul's joy run deeper than who the Philippians are in and of themselves or what they do for Paul. From the first verse of the letter, Paul indicates that to whom the Philippians belong is more important than who they are. Paul's joy arises from recognizing them "in Christ Jesus."

Paul commonly greets congregations by reminding them that he is an apostle. He addresses the Philippians as a slave in Christ Jesus. The New Revised Standard Version translates the word *douloi* as "servants" here, though it translates the same word as "slave" in 2:7 when referring to Jesus. Paul connects the status that he and Timothy share with the state Jesus enters as described in chapter 2. Christ shapes their living.

In Hellenistic culture, the status of an enslaved person was derived from the status of the owner. It was not just a matter of being a slave; it was a question of whose slave you were. When self-identifying as a slave, Paul attaches himself to the highest person, Jesus Christ (2:9-11). Christ, exalted above every other name in heaven and earth, forms the foundation of his identity. When Paul writes that he and Timothy are slaves in Christ Jesus, his point of emphasis lies in being "in Christ Jesus." Paul uses this phrase to describe a common relationship that he, Timothy, and the Philippians share, the status of being "in Christ Jesus." Their common relationship with Christ establishes a relationship with one another. Sharing in Christ Jesus forms the foundation of his joyful prayer.

Paul addresses the Philippians as "saints" in Christ Jesus. The quality of saint is not unique to this congregation. Paul addresses many of his letters to the "saints" in a certain city. *Hagiois* — "saints," or more literally, "holy ones" — was a common greeting among early Christians. Paul's use of the word *saints* need not evoke images of stained glass heroes or miracle-working figures. Paul does not think of the Philippians in an exalted state while he and Timothy share the lowly state of being slaves in Christ. Paul focuses not on the persons identified as saints but on the source of their sainthood: We are made saints in Christ Jesus. Paul is aware of shortcomings and struggles among these people. However, Christ calls them, and this calling makes them holy. As Karl Barth observes, "Holy people are unholy people" who have been claimed by God for God's purposes.[1] We encounter such holiness in Exodus 19 when God calls Israel holy because of its covenant relationship with God. At the heart of holiness or saintliness in the Bible, we find the idea of being in relationship with God and of letting this relationship shape our lives.

When I lose sight of who I am and who other people are "in Christ Jesus," my prayers focus on shortcomings I see in others, things that may annoy me about them or ways they do not measure up to my standards of who I think they ought to be. I see myself as better than or more than them. My intercessions become pleas for God to fix whatever I think is wrong with others, while my confessions sound more like the Pharisee in Luke 18:11, "God I thank you that I am not like. . . ." My prayers become rote recitations of illnesses, sins, my "to-do" list for God to fix. Sanctimonious ramblings make prayer a joyless discipline. Such prayer loses sight of God's grace working for good in our lives and the lives of those around us. Paul enters prayer by focusing on who we are in Christ Jesus. Beginning prayer like Paul turns it into a joyful discovery of what God is doing in our midst. Prayer becomes a joyful thanksgiving for how God works in the world.

Sharing in the Gospel

Paul gives thanks for how the Philippians have lived out this common relationship they have in Christ by "sharing in the gospel" (1:5). He remembers when they began this sharing and is thankful that it has continued into the present. *Koinonia*, the word translated "sharing" here, also appears in 1:7, 2:1, 3:10, 4:14. Paul talks of sharing in grace, suffering, work, and money. Most English translations of the New Testament render *koinonia* as "fellowship." Fred Craddock points out that *fellowship* may not be the best translation anymore: "For the church today to announce a

meeting for the purpose of fellowship is in essence to promise all attending that there will be no serious business, no
worship, no work."² That is, we use the word *fellowship* to
mean, "nothing important will happen here."

For Paul, fellowship is the gospel working itself out
in our lives. Fellowship is about with whom we associate
and what we try to accomplish together, how, and under
what conditions. Paul believes these matters go to the heart
of Christian living. Sharing together expresses our common identity as being "in Christ Jesus." Fellowship is not
optional in Paul's theology; it is not something in which we
choose whether to participate. To be in Christ Jesus is to be
connected to everyone who is in Christ Jesus. Even in times
of struggle and persecution, fellowship moves us to joyful
intercession for each other, as Christ prays for his disciples
before his betrayal. (See John 17.)

A few years ago, a friend shared with me the Ecumenical Prayer Cycle, a resource set up by the World Council
of Churches that assigns countries to a given week in the
year. Each week includes a brief description of the countries listed on the prayer cycle and information about what
is happening in churches within these countries. Needs for
prayer in each country and prayers from churches in some
of the countries are included each week.³ Incorporating

this cycle in my prayer time reminds me of the church universal, the common bond that we share with others united with Christ throughout the world. Many of these prayers joyfully express the good God is doing in these lands. Some of these Christians live and pray in situations where their faith in Christ puts their lives in danger, yet their prayers often express joyful participation in the work of the gospel. This discipline of praying for and with Christians around the world is a joyful celebration of our sharing together in Christ.

Confidence in God

Paul understands sharing together in the gospel as a sign of God at work in the Philippians. They have not achieved fellowship in Christ on their own. Recognizing God at work in the Philippians leads Paul to confident intercession for them. Like the psalmist, Paul is convinced that God's faithfulness in the past gives us hope for the future. He believes that the same God who called creation into being and raised Christ from the dead will not give up on the Philippians but will bring them to completion by the day of Jesus Christ.

Paul's joyful, constant prayer occurs while he is in prison. We do not expect to hear reports of joyful prayer from someone bound in chains for preaching the gospel. Just as Paul's joy is not based on what gifts he receives from the Philippians, neither is it rooted in his circumstances. Paul prays with joy not because he is on vacation at some resort. No, Paul prays joyfully for what God is doing in and through the Philippians while he is confined and persecuted. His viewing them in Christ Jesus allows Paul to be confident about what God will do among them, even though the Philippians also experience adverse circumstances.

Paul's thanksgiving for what God has done in the Philippians and his confidence that God is not done with them move him to intercede on their behalf. He expresses his confidence that God will cause them to grow in love until they can choose to act in ways that bring glory to God. So his intercession looks toward doxology, living for the glory of God.

Once I recognized Paul's pattern of moving from thanksgiving through intercession to doxology, I tried it in my own prayer life. I took the directory of the church I served at the time. Each day I prayed over five members in our congregation. With each name, I would find something in the person's life for which to give thanks and then would pray for God to continue to work in that person. Doing so was not always easy, but my prayers became more joyful.

Some names I did not recognize. I saw names that reminded me of conflicts or disagreements I had with members. But I was determined to pray with joy for all of them. Praying with joy did not mean that I would agree with everything about the person, what had been said or done, or even what the person thought about me. Joy at this point meant being able to find some sign that God was working in the person's life. I had to get to know some members better so I could find what God was doing in their lives. I saw my work like that of a detective; I searched for signs of how God had worked and was working in the lives of these people. I learned to spend more time listening in my prayers for what God might try to tell me about these people instead of telling God what I wanted to be sure God heard about them. Most importantly, I looked forward to this practice of prayer. I could not wait to see what names were next and what God might be doing in the lives of other members of the congregation.

It took me months of praying over five names every morning to work through the list. "God, thanks for what you have done in the life of . . . and for what you continue to do." My prayer was patterned and routine, but it led me to wonder at the mystery of God at work in our lives. I began each day joyfully anticipating this time in prayer. While I found different things in each person's past and present life for which to give thanks, I followed Paul's lead and offered a similar prayer for our common future of doxological living.

The Joy of Disciplined Prayer

Paul convinced me that many of my prayers are too anthropological. My prayers too easily go straight to intercessions or to confessions, things I want God to correct in other people or in me. Paul begins his prayer by giving thanks for what God has done, is doing, and will do among the Philippians. Petitions, intercessions, and confession are vital parts of prayer, but they are not the only parts. When our prayers focus only on human need and shortcomings, we lose our sense of awe and wonder at what God is doing in the world. Paul's letters follow a pattern: offering thanksgiving to God, addressing certain circumstances or issues in the church, and then closing with a doxology, a praise of God. Paul's letters became a pattern for my own prayer life: thanksgiving, intercession, confession, and praise. Paul's pattern of beginning and ending with attention on God helped me reframe my petitions for myself and others in light of who we are in God. I have found more at which to wonder in praise and more things for which to give God

WEEK ONE: JOYFUL PRAYER

thanks. Paul's words have given a more theological framework to my prayers.

My focus on human need without a theological framework of giving thanks and praise to God may have led to the lack of joy in my prayers. If our prayers focus only on human need and suffering, they easily become patterned around the same lists of hurts we want mended and failures we want rectified. When we surround our intercessions with thanksgiving for things God has already done and awe at who God is, they take on confidence and joy even in adverse situations.

Harvey Cox ends his book *A Feast of Fools* with a description of prayer as "disciplined fantasy." He describes thanksgiving as an act of play, as joy over something that has happened. He compares intercession to putting ourselves in someone else's situation. He defines penitence as imagining that we are not determined by our past. Cox calls this "disciplined fantasy" because these acts of prayer go against what we often take as common sense, as the way things are and the way things have to be. The term *fantasy* does not imply that thanksgiving, intercession, and penitence are made up through our brain power or wishful thinking. Part of the discipline comes from learning the stories of our faith, the way God has acted in the past and our hope for God's future. Cox believes that the resources of our faith and the discipline of structured practices of faith keep us looking and working toward God's future: "When the structure of a prayer is provided by ritual themes and historical images the prayer is a bridge to the future. It produces action toward a goal. It is not an escape from the world but the first step in its recreation."[4]

Paul taught me such "disciplined fantasy" through his joyful prayer for the Philippians. I looked forward to my time in prayer and did not dread it as a useful but dull routine. Paul helped me bridge a divide that had cut through my practice of prayer. I had struggled to claim my freedom and ability to form my prayers as I felt led and moved to do so, a style we call extemporaneous prayer. A problem arose: When I did not feel some pressing need or concern, I skipped my prayers or would find myself running through a familiar litany of prayer concerns. On the other hand, I was afraid using prayers out of a prayer book or fixed forms of prayer would begin to feel rote. Paul taught me a routine, a form of prayer that allowed flexibility and freedom. The form of moving from thanksgiving through petitions to doxology did not limit how I prayed for individuals or expressed praise to God. Having a form increased my sense of freedom in prayer.

In *Celebration of Discipline*, Richard Foster reminds us that joy is the keynote of all spiritual disciplines.[5] When we hear *spiritual disciplines*, we tend to think of forced practices meant to remove any sense of freedom and laughter from our lives. But when we practice discipline in our lives, we find a new sense of freedom from forces that once locked our spirits in resignation to "the way things are" and a sense of hopelessness. The joy of discipline moves us forward with hope. I discovered this hope through Paul's joyful prayer for the Philippians.

Perhaps during this season of Lent you could embark on an experiment with a new prayer discipline. You could adopt a form for your daily prayers similar to the one Paul uses for the Philippians. If you do not normally use a prayer book, try the practice of praying daily offices from a resource like the Book of Common Prayer or *Celtic Daily Prayers*.[6] The *Didache*, an early church manual, exhorted Christians to pray the Lord's Prayer three times a day. Perhaps you could reclaim this ancient prayer practice. Since the days of the early church, Christians have found strength and guidance in the discipline of prayer by praying through the Psalms. The Book of Common Prayer has a table of daily psalm readings that allows you to pray through the Psalms in a month. Use this season of Lent as a time to explore some of the joys of prayer that you may not have used previously or have forgotten about over the years. May this season of Lent be a time when you "constantly pray with joy" (Phil. 1:4).

DAILY SCRIPTURE READINGS

Romans 1:1-15	Psalm 2
1 Corinthians 1:1-9	Psalm 11
1 Thessalonians 1	Psalm 125

QUESTIONS FOR REFLECTION

1) Have you ever felt your prayers were dull, routine, a chore? If so, how did you pray during this time? What resources helped you or sustained your practice of prayer in this season?

2) What pattern helps structure your daily prayers like the pattern of thanksgiving, intercession, confession, and doxology that I shared? How does your prayer pattern provide a balance to order your thoughts and freedom of expression?

3) What new prayer disciplines are you incorporating as part of your observance of Lent? How has this new practice been difficult and uncomfortable? How has it produced joy and freedom in your prayer time?

4) What similarities and differences do you see in Paul's beginning to Philippians and the other letters listed in the daily scripture readings?

5) Which psalms do you find helpful in times of doubt, hurt, suffering, or persecution?

Week Two: Joyful Witness

Philippians 1:12-26

"I want you to know, beloved,
that what has happened to me
has actually helped to spread the gospel."
—Philippians 1:12

*G*ospel means "good news." The Greek word is *euange-lion*. The words *evangelist* and *evangelism* derive from this same Greek root. Remember, evangelism is about good news; it should be joyful.

Growing up, I was told that every Christian is called to be an evangelist, to spread the gospel. That idea scared me. The only evangelist I knew was Billy Graham, who would appear on television, preaching to large crowds in stadiums

BECAUSE OF THIS I REJOICE

in foreign countries. I was not even sure God wanted me to preach, but I was pretty sure I did not want to preach to mass crowds in foreign countries. I was willing to entertain the idea that God might call me to preach, but I was feeling no call to be an evangelist like Billy Graham. Evangelism, as I understood it, terrified me.

I later learned of a few evangelism programs that some churches use to train members. These efforts did not help my understanding of evangelism. Some of these programs focused more on bad news than good news. They highlighted sin and the threat of future punishment. Such evangelism seemed long on diagnosing evil and short on celebrating the glad news of what God does in Jesus Christ.

The most popular form of evangelism I encountered as a boy involved sharing a testimony or witness. These witnesses often related an experience of reaching desperate situations and then turning to Jesus to have life fixed. They reminded me of Paul on the road to Damascus in Acts 9. They did not include anyone falling off a horse or being blinded, but they usually mentioned a bright light when Jesus appeared followed by some significant change in lifestyle for the person telling the story. They were stories of dramatic conversions. Often the person was in jail because of drugs or alcohol, and they encountered Jesus, who helped them leave jail a changed person. I thought I would never have a witness because my mom was determined to keep me out of any trouble. How was I going to have a life-changing encounter with Jesus that could lead to a witness if my mother was convinced I always had to be good?

My apprehensions about evangelism reached a turning point on a school bus. When I was in the third grade, my friend Jon sat next to me on the bus one morning and asked, "What's your witness?" Since this was not his usual greeting, I was confused. A heavy dose of fear followed the confusion. I thought, *I have not lived long enough to do enough bad things yet for Jesus to rescue me. How can I have a witness?*

I blurted out something about knowing Jesus loved me and cared for me, even though he was aware of bad things I did. It was not poetic. The clouds did not part to reveal me surrounded by some bright light. Jon's eyesight never faltered. Nobody even fell off their seat onto the floor of the bus. I was sure I messed it up. Whatever I had done, I was certain it was not a witness. It was not like any of the testimonies I heard in church.

After a few minutes, Jon said, "Well, that seems like something worth knowing. Tell me more about how you know Jesus loves you." I do not know what else I said that morning, but I remember that I enjoyed talking to my friend about Jesus. A few years later, while going through confirmation, I shared this story with my father. He said, "Sounds like evangelism to me."

Many of us struggle with evangelism because of stereotypes and misunderstandings of evangelism.[1] We fear it coerces people into faith. Perhaps we have endured membership recruitment techniques that were falsely labeled evangelism. Maybe we do not understand the difference between those who are gifted with the call to give their lives to evangelistic ministries and the calling that all Christians have to bear witness to Jesus Christ. While passages like Matthew 28:16-20 and Acts 1:8 speak about the responsibility of every disciple to bear witness to Jesus, Ephesians 4:11-12 reminds us that the Spirit has given some Christians a gift to spread the gospel. These "gifted" evangelists have a special ability and call to share the gospel with people as they go about daily living. However, willingness to witness to the gospel is an expectation of all disciples of Jesus.

Remember, the gospel is good news. Sharing good news is a joyous experience. We need not dread evangelism. Paul offers a joyful witness and believes that whatever the future holds, he will continue to rejoice in witnessing.

In That I Rejoice

When preaching on one of Paul's letters written from prison, I often joke with the congregation I serve that few of them would be surprised to learn if I were imprisoned. I hope, though, that they would ask how I was doing in jail. The Philippians know that Paul is in prison. They expect to hear about his imprisonment in his letter. So, after reporting on his prayers for them, Paul turns to his imprisonment. However, he shares little about his circumstances. Instead, he says his imprisonment helps advance the gospel. It allows him to preach to a new audience of guards and Roman officials. The gospel advances, and Paul rejoices.

Paul may be jailed, but the gospel is free. Paul does not say whether his testimony is through his legal witness or whether others are attracted to how he conducts himself while confined. For Paul, these new circumstances provide a new opportunity to share the gospel. Everyone knows that he is confined for his faith in Jesus. The Philippians want to know how things are with Paul. Paul wants them to know how things are with the gospel.

Paul's confinement encourages other Christians to witness. Some, seeing Paul in prison and understanding that he stands trial for the gospel, preach Christ in places Paul can no longer visit. These Christians gain confidence through Paul's example of joyful jail-bound witness. Others, Paul says, preach Christ out of rivalry, hoping to increase Paul's suffering through their preaching. Perhaps these other preachers use Paul's imprisonment as grounds to discredit him and cause people to doubt his preaching. Robert Jewett believes these other preachers promote a gospel of glory: teaching that believers will always live victoriously and not endure suffering.[2] According to such teaching, Paul's imprisonment indicates that he must be either in error or not of true faith. We cannot know the nature of this selfish ambition and rivalry to which Paul alludes because, for Paul, it does not matter. Paul cares that persons and their actions preach Jesus. Jesus, not Paul, is the subject of Christian witness.

The Philippians may not question why Paul is in prison and others around Paul may be moved out of love to share the gospel more boldly, but most of us want an explanation when we hear that a clergy person is in jail. My joking with our congregation aside, I am sure they would want to know the reason if I did wind up in jail. On Good Friday, April 12, 1963, Martin Luther King Jr. was arrested and placed in jail in Birmingham, Alabama. That same day, a "Call for Unity" appeared in local papers. The "Call," written by local white clergy leaders, denounced the nonviolent protests for which Civil Rights activists like King called in Birmingham. They considered leaders of the protest "outside agitators." They believed local citizens, black and white, should work for resolutions within legal means. On April 10, a circuit judge placed a blanket injunction on any further marches. By marching on April 12, King, an outside agitator, disobeyed the law.

King read the "Call for Unity" in his jail cell. On the margins of the article and scraps of paper, King penned a response. His "Letter from a Birmingham Jail" acknowledges that he usually does not respond to his critics. However, since he considers these clergymen brothers and fears others may use his imprisonment to discredit the Civil Rights Movement, he feels he must respond. King closes his letter hoping that one day he and the authors of the "Call to Unity" will sit together in Christian fellowship. Throughout the letter, King is honest about his differences with these other clergy regarding how racial equality and justice can occur in Birmingham. Though he recognizes them as detractors of the methods he advocates, he reaches out to them as allies in the cause. While King rankles at their labeling him and his associates "outside agitators," he believes that an underlying bond holds them together, a bond stronger than these painful differences.

King tells this story in his book *Why We Can't Wait*.[3] When discerning whether to participate in the Good Friday march, he and Ralph Abernathy decided they "would present our bodies as personal witnesses."[4] King silences any detractors of the Civil Rights Movement and reminds us that such civil disobedience goes back to the days of Shadrach, Meshach, and Abednego in the Old Testament through the witness of the martyrs who "rejoiced at being deemed worthy to suffer for what they believed."[5] Jail has produced some great opportunities to witness to the gospel, and Paul, writing from his jail cell, teaches about witnessing joyfully as a spiritual discipline.

Witnessing as a Spiritual Discipline

We do not think of evangelism as a spiritual discipline as readily as we think of reading the Bible, fasting, or prayer. These other activities develop our personal relationship with God. Witnessing has an external focus: sharing God with others. When evangelism centers on the evangelist, we lose sight of the joy of the gospel. Much of my early struggle with witnessing arose from my focus on myself: what I needed to say, do, sound like, or look like. Yet Paul offers us an example of how to discipline our witness so that God is the subject who invites us to participate in telling our story to achieve what God wants to accomplish. Then witnessing becomes a way to grow in our awareness of God's presence in the world. A focus on sharing the good news of God's work in the world frees us for joyful witness.

Paul shows that we do not have to create occasions or special circumstances to share the gospel. We can share it anywhere. Some of the best evangelism we can offer comes from sharing how responding to the gospel directs our daily decisions. Paul did not go to jail so he could share the gospel with Roman guards, but, once there, he uses the occasion to witness.

Paul celebrates more than his witness. He rejoices in the witness others offer as well. We do not have to confine our witness to only the things God is doing in our lives. We can witness by joyfully sharing what God is doing in other Christians, other churches, other ministries, and other parts of the world. Limiting our witness to our personal encounter with Jesus may still direct too much attention to ourselves rather than to the larger story of God's work in the world.

By disciplining ourselves to concentrate more on Christ as the subject of our witness and by using everyday events and circumstances to relate to others how our commitment to Christ impacts decisions in our life, we grow in our ability and opportunities to witness. We do not need to blow a trumpet every time we write a check to support some ministry or spend a Saturday working at a local food bank. People will ask. They will want to know why we spend part of Sunday in worship. Someone will ask what we did with our Saturday and why. Sharing how these actions help us respond to God rather than what they say about us brings us to the heart of witness.

Like Paul, our witness changes in different times and circumstances. The dramatic testimonies I heard growing up hardly ever changed. After someone began a testimony, almost anyone could have finished it. It was the same story over and over again. It started and stopped at the same place. It lacked a sense of progress. What happens after meeting Jesus and leaving jail? How does life change? Paul is not content to let his witness stand fixed in time. He looks forward to rejoicing by witnessing in other circumstances.

And I Will Rejoice

Paul's thought transitions from present to future tense in verse 18. He shifts from rejoicing about the ways Christ has been and is being shared to hoping for a future joyful spread of the gospel. No matter what happens, Christ will be shared. Despite Paul's focus on preaching Christ, he does not slip into universalism by celebrating the evangelism of his detractors. In chapter 3, he engages in vigorous debate with those he thinks are not preaching the gospel. He does not say, "It does not matter what we believe, so long as we believe." Nor does Paul adopt an attitude of, "Well, it does not matter what they teach as long as their hearts are right." Paul insists they preach from bad motives. However, they preach Christ, and, for Paul, that is what matters. So he rejoices. As the gospel advances, he believes he will continue to rejoice. Paul is not concerned whether he dies in jail or is released and returns to the Philippians. Paul implores the Philippians to pray for his boldness to witness in life or in death. Just as he prayed that God would continue to work through the Philippians, Paul asks that they intercede regarding his future witness. His faithful witness is more important than life or death.

The Greek word for "witness" is *martyr*. In later centuries, the church identified as martyrs those Christians who gave the ultimate witness by suffering and dying for their faith in Jesus. This distinction had not been made by the time Paul writes to the Philippians. Paul says we are all martyrs, witnesses to Jesus Christ, whether through our life or our death. The witness of other Christians can inspire us to joyful witness. Paul provides an example of faithful, joyful witness for the Philippians as they too experience persecution. His joyful witness will inspire the Philippians to continue their joyful witness.

Years ago I was leading a class on faith-sharing. A young newlywed couple in the class attended enthusiastically and studied diligently. Each week they showed up with lots of questions. Though committed to a life of discipleship, they shared openly their struggle with how to witness to their faith. They feared sharing their faith meant imposing their beliefs on others. About halfway through the course, they called and asked to meet with me before our next session. I thought they were coming to tell me they were leaving the class. They walked into my office and said, "We think we shared our faith. We want to know if we did it right, and we are not comfortable sharing this experience with others in the group."

I decided not to tell them my misgivings about being a good judge in the matter of what counts as evangelism as I had not realized I had witnessed to my best friend on a school bus. "Tell me what happened," I said.

"We bought a car," they replied.

This statement did not seem a great beginning to a story about witnessing. My mind flooded with the harmful messages of the prosperity gospel and "God loves me, so I drive an expensive car." When they told me they thought that they had witnessed during the financing, I wondered how I could ask them to leave the class.

The loan officer informed them they qualified for a more expensive car than what they had budgeted. They asked how he had reached his conclusion. They compared their budget with the loan officer's information. Their income was the same. Their estimated bills were roughly the same. But the loan officer estimated more disposable income than they had in their budget. As they looked over the loan officer's list of bills and expenditures, one of them noticed that their tithe was not listed. They explained the missing information and that, for them, tithing was a commitment they would not break; it was how they helped support the ministry of their church.

"This is the other reason we wanted to talk to you," they said. "First, we are not sure that we witnessed. Second, we do not want to sound like we are bragging about what we give the church."

I thanked them for their humility and said I thought they had indeed shared how their commitment to live as disciples of Jesus Christ impacts their daily life. They did not seek out this opportunity. They did not go into a car dealership with the intent to evangelize anyone. But when the chance came to witness to how they make financial decisions, they shared their faith. They would be the last people to offer up their car-buying experience as a model Christian witness, but it was a start. As my dad said: Sounds like evangelism to me.

Jesus says not to worry about what to say or how to say it or when it will happen. When we need to witness to him, we trust the Spirit to help us find our way. (See Mark 13:11.) Our disciplines of paying attention to God's working in our lives and the lives of others gives content to our testimonies. As we continue through Lent, let's open ourselves to joyfully share with others how the gospel shapes lives.

DAILY SCRIPTURE READINGS

Matthew 28:16-20	John 14:15-31
Mark 16:14-20	John 15:18-27
Luke 24:36-49	John 16:1-15

QUESTIONS FOR REFLECTION

1) What do the words *evangelism* and *witness* bring to mind for you? Which one of these words is more comfortable for you than the other? Why?

3) How are your memories and ideas of evangelism joyful or painful for you?

4) Consider your personal daily activities. What parts of your day are ordered by your commitment to Jesus?

5) When have you been surprised by an unexpected opportunity to witness?

6) How can you share what God is doing in the life of your church?

Week Three: Joyful Humility

Philippians 1:27–2:18

"Make my joy complete."
—Philippians 2:2

I still remember sitting in a lecture room on the campus of Wofford College in the spring of 1989. Half of me listened as Dr. Charlie Barrett talked about the benefits of studying Christian theology. The other half looked out the window and thought of baseball, golf, and other springtime activities. Then Dr. Barrett uttered something that hit me like a thunderbolt, reclaiming all my attention. He said he hoped one day to reach the humility of Brother Lawrence of the Resurrection. Lawrence taught him that humility comes through doing even the simplest task to honor God. Doing anything to honor God gives the task dignity and purpose. Thus, nothing is beneath us. With a posture like Brother Lawrence, we will not be tempted to think someone else should do a task because we are too important to do it.

I had considered Dr. Barrett the humblest person I knew. If he hoped one day to reach the type of humility of this Brother Lawrence, I needed to know more about Lawrence. That afternoon, I found a copy of *The Practice of the Presence of God*, a collection of Lawrence's letters, maxims, and conversations compiled by those who sought spiritual guidance from Lawrence.[1]

Brother Lawrence was a lay member of a monastic community in seventeenth-century France. His first assignment was to work in the kitchen. Later, due to pain in his leg, he worked in the shoe shop where he could sit through his labor. Lawrence performed some of the lowest tasks in the monastery, but he developed a reputation for carrying out his assignments without complaints despite his suffering. His reputation spread outside the monastery so that priests, nuns, and church officials came to him for spiritual guidance. To those who visited Lawrence and asked how he could face his work with such good spirits, his refrain became that he tried to carry out each task, no matter how

great or small, as if done in the presence of God. This awareness of God's presence marked his life with humility.

Gospel Lives

Paul believes such humility marks genuine Christian community. After reporting on his prayer for the Philippians
and the situation of the gospel, Paul turns in Philippians
1:27 to the congregation's situation. How are things going
with them? And how should they be living?

Paul has asked the Philippians to pray that he continues
to witness faithfully to the gospel in the face of opposition.
He now speaks of opponents they face and their struggling
for the gospel. He calls them to faithful witness through
living together humbly.

Paul places the Philippians' suffering in the context of the
cross. They have the privilege of suffering for Christ. Grace
and suffering seem an unlikely combination. Like Paul's
detractors, there are still those who teach that our lives will
be free of pain and suffering if we believe in Jesus. But Paul
says God grants the privilege of suffering to believers. The
Christian life is not an escape from this world; the Christian
life brings the joy of the gospel into the pain and suffering of the world. Compassion motivates Jesus to minister.

Compassion means "suffering with." Since the Christian life flows from the life of Christ, we can expect not only to suffer in our life but also to enter into others' suffering. Paul's talk of joy is not a denial of suffering but a witness to suffering from its very center—the cross. Christians who enter the pain of the world most deeply often express Christian living most joyfully. Saint Francis ministered to pain so profoundly that he reportedly bore in his body the *stigmata*, the marks of Christ's suffering on the cross. Yet Francis, as H. A. Williams reminds us, is also remembered as one of the most jovial Christians.[2]

Paul warns the Philippians not to let suffering and persecution destroy their unity. This unity is a faithful witness. Rather than turning against one another when trouble and hardships arise or abandoning one another amid persecution, Paul encourages them to turn toward one another with support and acts of helpful service, especially in times of distress. Humility encourages us to serve one another and maintain unity in the face of hardship. Paul does not lift up a negative conception of unity built around a shared, mutual enemy. Such unity disappears when the opponent does. Paul says to live out of the unity that comes from a shared pursuit of a gospel-worthy life. To live worthy of the gospel is to live out of the common bond we have in

Christ. The same fellowship that connects the Philippians to Paul works itself out in acts of mutual care and support.

Paul calls us to live grace under pressure. First, he says, count it grace to suffer for the faith. Doing so puts us in good company with people like Paul and Jesus. Second, we have the fellowship of the church to strengthen and support us. This fellowship calls us to suffer with and for others. We do not make such humility happen through moral effort. Rather, the type of humility to which Paul calls us comes when we let the gospel work itself out in our lives. Our relationship with Christ calls us to live not by reacting to whatever opposition confronts us but out of the active power of the gospel at work within us. This way of living out the gospel marks our lives with joy despite suffering.

In "Joy in Praise," James O'Mahony speaks about the "suavity of joy."[3] He says that when joy is a part of our lives, it animates us in such a way that the word *joy* can describe our movements in the same way the word *grace* can describe the movements of a dancer or an athlete. Paul has something like "suavity of joy" in mind in his call for us to set loose the life Jesus grants us—a life worthy of the gospel. We cannot construct this life through our work. A life lived worthy of the gospel expresses God's working in and through us.

Complete My Joy

Philippians 2 opens with a practical picture of the unity Paul has in mind. This unity grows out of what we experience in Christ: encouragement, consolation, fellowship in the Spirit, and compassion. These experiences find expression in a common life marked by a unified mind, love, spirit, and purpose. Life based on the gospel connects Christians to one another. Such unity is part of the witness of the church.

The opposite of the unity Paul pictures is a community marked by selfish ambition and conceit. Disunity strikes at the heart of Paul's understanding of fellowship. To be in fellowship and to express fellowship means to find concrete expressions of grace in our neighbor. Concern with proving oneself right or trying to put oneself above someone else is the very opposite of this humility. Humility lives for the glory of God, not self.[4]

Paul promotes not self-deprecation but recognition of the grace of God active in the life of our neighbors. Paul calls us to humble ourselves not only before those we like, who we think like us, or who practice their faith the way we do. Paul calls us to humble ourselves before those who annoy us, who have habits that disturb us, or who have a different viewpoint than ours. Humility puts the interest of others before self-interest. As Barth says in his commentary on this passage, "Humility *in abstracto* can be the grossest pride."[5] We do not commit to the idea, much less the ideal, of humility. We commit to the flesh and blood humility that greets us in our neighbor. Marked by such a common life, a community of Christians can unite despite differences. Outsiders observing such a common life will recognize it as different from other types of community.

Outsiders often name religious groups. Acts 11 tells how the disciples were first called Christians in Antioch. While the early followers of Jesus referred to themselves as people of the Way or disciples, outsiders noticed their life together. Since they lived as if they were slaves of this Christ they talked about, they called them Christians. John Wesley and his friends at Oxford were first called Methodists by those mocking the rigid methods they followed in Christian living. The outsiders who called the early followers of Jesus Christians and the Oxford students who called Wesley and his friends Methodists observed something different about these groups. They may have named them mockingly, but their mocking stemmed from their observation of those who humbled themselves before the needs of their neighbors. Christian unity expresses itself through mutual care and service.

BECAUSE OF THIS I REJOICE

Others may not ask us to share a personal witness, but they observe us. We witness to those around us whether verbally or nonverbally. One vital witness the church gives is humble service to one another. Friedrich Nietzsche reportedly said he would believe in the Redeemer when Christians lived as if they were redeemed. His challenge applies as much to the life of the church as a fellowship as it does to our personal lives. Paul's joy will find completion in the church's faithful continuance of joyful humility exhibited through humble service.

The Christ Jesus Mindset

For many modern interpreters, Philippians 2:6-11 forms the heart of Paul's appeal to the congregation. Since the early twentieth century, most scholars agree that these verses are an early Christian hymn, a poetic piece that stands out from the prose surrounding it. Some think it may have been an early creed rather than a song. Most agree that this hymn predates Paul but that Paul inserts the line about the cross in verse 8, which disrupts the rhythm of the passage. Paul's theology centers on the cross and resurrection, which transforms the cross into a symbol of hope. Through the resurrection, Christ empowers us to live transformed and transformative lives in the suffering of the world. It would be just like Paul to insert the cross into this poem.

But why does Paul insert this poem into his letter? Why does he place it at this point in his argument? For that, we have to go back to his introduction to the hymn. In Philippians 2:5, Paul admonishes us to live out the mind we have in Christ Jesus. Recall his greeting in the first verse of the letter: Paul introduces himself and Timothy and greets the Philippians as those who are "in Christ Jesus." He calls the Philippians saints in Christ and identifies himself as a slave in Christ. Our common placement in Christ unites us and enables us to live humbly with one another.

The hymn then lays out the Christ Jesus mindset out of which Christians are to live. Verses 6-8 describe Christ's descent from the glories of God's presence to the depths of death on a cross. Through this descent, Christ appears in the form of a slave. His slavery represents his giving up any claim to God's form. Christ's form is humble, self-denying, and self-sacrificing, and Paul wants us to emulate it. Christian unity grows through Christ-like humility. Such unity is more than getting our doctrines to agree or an emotional affiliation. Christian unity comes by living together in self-giving service.

The second part of the hymn (vv. 9-11) celebrates God's exaltation of Christ after his death on the cross. Our strength for living comes from Christ's place of exaltation. Paul calls us to live according to the resources Jesus offers us. Humble, mutual service is possible because Christ puts it at our disposal, not because we achieve it on our own. John 13:1-20 illustrates concretely the Christ Jesus mindset. As Jesus and the disciples gather for their last meal, Jesus takes a towel and water to clean the disciples' feet. He places himself in a posture of service to the disciples as he performs work usually assigned to slaves. Peter protests, but Jesus says, "I am doing this as an example of how you should treat one another" (John 13:15, AP). Paul says we now have the mindset to live such humble acts in service to one another.

My last semester in seminary, I attended a seminar taught by Tom Langford. Dr. Langford was a great scholar and a gifted teacher. Through most of my time at Duke Divinity School, he served as provost to the university and did not teach. When he finally taught a class, I felt privileged to be able to enroll. The first day of the seminar, Dr. Langford sat down and shared a couple of paragraphs he had written. Once done, he asked us for questions and comments. I was so mesmerized by the poetry of what Langford shared that I could not formulate any response. Another student blurted out a question that I thought was the most simplistic, waste-of-time question anyone could have uttered. I became angry that anyone would waste the great Dr. Langford's time with such nonsense. I wanted to scream, "Please don't squander your time responding to that question!" However, Dr. Langford noted the question and then continued listening and responding to each student. He treated every person with respect and every question with thoughtfulness. In the process, he washed away my intellectual pride and vanity, and I found the voice to participate in the community of scholars he was building. His humility showed me how to learn as much from my colleagues as from his wisdom.

Give Salvation a Workout

Philippians 2:12-18 calls us to work out our salvation with fear and trembling. Paul does not mean each of us needs to sit down with our Bible and figure out this whole salvation thing as best we can, though many interpret the passage this way. Paul still speaks in the plural here. He says you *all* work this out. By *work out*, a phrase which might at first seem like an idea of salvation that we have to earn or achieve, Paul means, "let your salvation be shown in your life together." It's like a soccer team running drills during practice, training their muscles and reflexes to work in harmony, only the practice field is life, the team is Christian community, and the muscles are salvation. Finally, by placing this workout in the context of fear and trembling, Paul reminds us that we carry out our work together before God. In the Bible, the words *fear* and *trembling* denote standing in the presence of God. Paul does not ask us to figure out our salvation or fear the consequences. Instead, he calls us to let the salvation God offers work itself out in our life together. Paul's admonition to fear and trembling is the same as Brother Lawrence's call to practicing the presence of God: Our faith calls us to live our lives directed toward the glory of God.

While Paul calls for this corporate humility among Christians, he does not mean for it to be kept secret from the world. We offer corporate witness to the world through our public displays of mutual humility. Or, as Paul puts it, we shine like stars amid a crooked and perverse generation. Our luminescence is no cause for pride on our part because only God's working through us makes it possible.

Paul describes the Philippians' witness as an offering and his witness as a libation. He intends both acts of sacrifice to be carried out in joy. Paul does not say, "Do this so that one day you will experience joy," but, rather, "Carry out this offering with joy, put your faith to work in living joyfully together." When we joyfully serve one another in humility, our salvation grows stronger.

Humility does not have to occur in spectacular acts of witness like martyrs facing wild animals or gladiators. Humility can come through mutual service that provides meals to those who are suffering, visits the sick and does not neglect them, and provides food to the hungry. Humility offers such acts of kindness not just for those we like or who we feel deserve such acts but to anyone with whom we are connected in Christ. We do such humble acts for those with whom we disagree as well as for those who always seem to agree with us. Humility enables us to live together in such a way that others see our life as something different from what they have come to expect in the world and to do so fueled by joy.

I worked with a team in Honduras to rebuild a Methodist church destroyed by a hurricane one summer. I speak and understand very little Spanish. Members of the local Methodist church would join us in our work when they were able. They taught us to sing the first verse of "De Colores" in Spanish. We taught them to sing the first verse of "Amazing Grace" in English. We would sing as we carried cement blocks across a creek to the building site. Some days we sang those songs more times than I could count. While we sang, worked, laughed, and smiled together, others would stop and notice us. I do not think they stopped because the singing was so melodious. I think they stopped because they saw us joyfully serving with one another despite our differences.

DAILY SCRIPTURE READINGS

Psalm 1	Galatians 3:1-14
John 13:1-20	Galatians 6:1-10
John 13:31-35	James 2:14-26

QUESTIONS FOR REFLECTION

1) Who comes to mind when you hear the word humility? In what ways do they illustrate humility?

2) Think about someone you know who is willing to enter into the pain and suffering of others. Does this service seem like an obligation or a joyful expression of humility?

3) How can a Christian community bear witness to the gospel? How does our life together share our Christian faith with the world?

4) When has the witness of the church failed to be "worthy of the gospel"?

5) What does it mean to you to work out your salvation with fear and trembling?

Week Four: Joyful Hospitality

Philippians 2:19-30

"Welcome him then in the Lord with all joy,
and honor such people."
—Philippians 2:29

In a second-century letter, the philosopher Lucian ridicules the early Christians for their hospitality. Lucian relates how Christians surround the Cynic philosopher Peregrinus with support when Peregrinus is imprisoned while pretending to be a Christian. Lucian attacks Peregrinus as an opportunist and a charlatan, and he makes fun of the Christians for the expense and encouragement they offer Peregrinus, who is a prisoner and largely unknown to the Christians:

> Well, when he had been imprisoned, the Christians, regarding the incident as a calamity, left nothing undone in the effort to rescue him[.] Then, as this was impossible, every other form of attention was shown him, not in any casual way but with assiduity, and from the very break of day aged widows and orphan children could be seen waiting near the prison, while their officials even slept inside with him after bribing the guards.[1]

Lucian's satire of Christian hospitality illustrates how vital this discipline was to early Christians.

Hospitality helped grow the early church.[2] Members with large houses provided the first gathering places for congregations. With few inns for travelers, early Christian missionaries relied on other Christians opening their homes to them as they traveled between congregations in different towns. We see this reflected in the instructions Jesus gives to the disciples regarding their missionary journeys. (See Mark 6:7-13.) Jesus sends the disciples out with an expectation of hospitality. We read injunctions in Romans 12:13 and 1 Peter 4:9 about entertaining other Christians. Hebrews 13:2 reminds us that hospitality allows some to entertain angels without realizing it. Hospitality becomes one of the responsibilities of church leaders by the time some of the latest New Testament books are written. (See 1 Timothy 5:10 and Titus 1:8.)

The *Didache*, written toward the end of the first century, gives instructions for extending hospitality to others. It says to welcome missionaries and traveling Christians for two to three days and then to send them on their way. Apparently, the writer of the *Didache* believed that missionaries, like fish and other visitors, begin to smell after three days.[3]

Hospitality was important since new believers were often ostracized by family members and friends. For such converts, the church became their new social system. In the New Testament, believers use familial language with one another. Church members become brothers and sisters in Christ.

Paul relies on Christian hospitality in his oversight and communication with churches. When he cannot visit a church due to imprisonment or work that detains him, he deploys his associates to take his instructions to other congregations and bring back news of their progress in the faith. These associates carry Paul's letters and implement any corrections Paul wants to take place in the congregations. Thus, we often find words of commendation for these associates in his letters.

Though Paul hopes to revisit the Philippians, his future remains unknown. He will send Timothy to them once his outcome is determined. In the meantime, he sends Epaphroditus back to them. Paul shares his joy in sending such faithful companions to minister in Philippi during his absence. He wants the Philippians to receive them joyfully as an expression of the Christian hospitality that helps spread the gospel.

My Son Timothy

Paul cannot wait to hear how the Philippians are doing. He plans to send his associate Timothy to visit them and send word back to Paul about their condition. Paul introduces Timothy at the beginning of the letter as his fellow slave in Christ Jesus. Now he reminds the Philippians of the deep connection and affection that he has for Timothy and Timothy has for them. Paul describes Timothy as his son and says Timothy shares Paul's longing and desire for the Philippians.[4]

Timothy was with Paul when he founded the church in Philippi. (See Acts 16.) The Philippians already know his character and do not need Paul to recommend him. But they may not realize that Timothy exemplifies the very type of self-denying humility that Paul has just exhorted them to offer one another. He describes Timothy as one who puts the interests of Christ above his own interest. In sending Timothy to them, Paul gives a living example of the type of service he hopes the Philippians will offer one another.

More important than Timothy's feelings for the Philippians or the example that he offers of self-giving service is Paul's sending him "in the Lord Jesus." This phrase modifies Paul's hope of sending Timothy to them. Paul's "hope in the Lord Jesus" conveys more than, "If the Lord wills, I will be able to send Timothy to you." Paul's phrasing indicates that believers are to put all of life at the Lord's disposal. Paul and Timothy submit to Christ's lordship in their plans and their actions. As Paul sends Timothy in the Lord, the Philippians should receive him in the Lord. They do not need to fear Timothy as an enforcer sent by Paul to straighten out their behavior. He comes to share with them in the Lord. Rather than being a burden, Timothy's visit is a further sharing in Christian ministry.

In the early church, welcoming a Christian brother or sister is akin to welcoming Christ. This idea goes back to the Old Testament with stories like Abraham welcoming God by offering hospitality to three strangers. (See Genesis 18:1-8.) The writer of Hebrews exhorts early

Christians to extend such hospitality to strangers because some have entertained angels unknowingly (Hebrews 13:2). Jesus' refrain in Matthew 25:31-46 reiterates the point: "When you have done it to one of the least of these, you have done it unto me" (AP).

The legend of Martin of Tours exemplifies how we encounter Christ when we offer hospitality to others. While Martin is still a catechumen and serving in the Roman army, he encounters a beggar lying by the city wall. He dismounts his horse, cuts his military cloak in half, and gives half to the beggar. During the night, Martin has a vision of Christ walking through heaven wearing half of his cloak. When the angels ask why Jesus will not remove the garment, Jesus replies, "Because my servant Martin gave it to me" (AP).[5]

John Wesley wrote a sermon based on the parable in Matthew 25 entitled, "On Visiting the Sick."[6] In the sermon, Wesley calls acts of mercy a means of grace, a place and act where we expect to encounter God. When I first read Wesley's premise, it turned my understanding of mission work upside down. For years I had engaged in acts of mercy with the attitude that Christians need to supply others out of our abundance. However, Wesley says that acts of mercy like visiting the sick or those in prison, feeding the hungry, and clothing the naked sanctify *us*. Rather than carrying out these practices as though we have all the faith and resources and others are fortunate to benefit from our excess, Wesley encourages us to do these works of mercy expecting to encounter Christ in those we serve. When we share with others our experiences in mission and service ministries, we often express this holy encounter with the common saying, "I received much more than I gave."

Your Apostle Epaphroditus

Paul will wait to know his outcome before sending Timothy. For now, he returns Epaphroditus to the Philippians. Epaphroditus was their messenger to Paul. He likely brought the gift the Philippians sent to aid Paul while he was in prison. He may have been part of their gift, expected to stay with and minister to Paul in prison. Paul calls him the apostle—one sent to represent another—of the Philippians. Paul returns Epaphroditus to the Philippians as Paul's apostle: He brings with him Paul's letter until Timothy can return to them.

At some point in serving Paul, Epaphroditus has been sick. The Philippians hear of his illness and worry. Epaphroditus learns that his home congregation worries about him, and he becomes anxious about their concern. They have had good reason for concern: Epaphroditus had been near death. Now their friend and messenger is okay, and Paul thinks sending Epaphroditus back to the Philippians is best. Paul hopes to relieve their anxiety for their messenger and the anxiety Epaphroditus has for them.

Paul expects the Philippians to welcome Epaphroditus joyfully, more than a friend returned from a long journey or recovered from serious illness. Paul describes Epaphroditus's ministry as a priestly sacrifice, which recalls Paul's libation and his calls for the Philippians to live sacrificially. Epaphroditus also exemplifies the self-denying humility that Paul believes is at the heart of Christian living. Epaphroditus risked his life in rendering service to Paul. He should be welcomed back joyfully and as a hero of the faith, not because of what he did for Paul but because of how he was willing to give of himself to the point of death for Christ. Epaphroditus returns home not because he could not complete his assignment or has become homesick. Paul affirms Epaphroditus's status as Paul's brother, his fellow laborer in the gospel, and a soldier who stood his post. Thus the Philippians can welcome him with full joy.

The congregation I serve hosts five or six young adult missionaries for a Sunday each August. They visit us as they finish their training and prepare to serve for two years in domestic or foreign mission locations. We love hearing about their call to mission work and about where they will serve in ministry. We look forward to praying for them and hearing from them once they go to their assignments. Each group visit reminds us that we are part of the work that goes on in the places they will serve. Their stories of call and service open our minds and hearts to new ways we can do ministry in our context. They cause some of our members to ask whether they may be called to missionary service. At first, we thought we were being nice and giving these new missionaries a place to speak on a Sunday. But after extending hospitality, we found ourselves called to new expressions of joyful ministry and to rejoice in the work God is doing around the world.

The Discipline of Joyful Hospitality

The expectation of encountering God in joyful hospitality fueled the early church in living out this discipline, and it helped the joyous spread of the gospel. Yet for some of us, hospitality may evoke ideas of rigid etiquette rules and guests who never leave. Hospitality can seem more like a test of our patience than a practice of growing closer to God. I felt this way for a long time.

When Kristen and I were engaged, I worked at a church where I taught and occasionally preached. My primary responsibility at this church was teaching a class entitled "Discovering Your Spiritual Gifts" to as many members as possible. I taught the class on Wednesday nights; I taught it to various Sunday School classes; I taught half-day retreats on the material. New ministries came out of these classes as members saw how their gifts complemented one another, and they gathered around shared passions. I taught the class fifteen times in a two-year period. Kristen attended three or four of these sessions. (I still do not know how she sat through multiple offerings of this class.)

The class included an inventory similar to personality inventories but designed to help individuals discover where they felt best equipped to serve in ministry. I reminded participants that the goal of the inventory was to discover the three or four spiritual gifts that rated highest for each of them. Hopefully this would help them discern where they were best equipped to serve in ministry. I also reminded participants that scores in the inventory could not be used as comparisons, either with other members or individually. Everyone would have some gifts that ranked high, many in the middle, and some gifts that ranked low. Low rankings do not imply deficiency as a Christian; everyone will have low-ranked gifts. However, we would not want to put someone who ranked lowest in evangelism over that whole ministry area. Each person has some gift for ministry; we just need to find the right place for each person.

This understanding of spiritual gifts made sense to me. I used a series of Bible passages to teach where we got this understanding from scripture. Each time I led a group through the material, I would take the spiritual gifts inventory with the participants. I helped others live into claiming their gifts and found my own sense of calling strengthened and affirmed. The trouble was, every time I took the survey, hospitality ranked dead last. While my top three gifts were consistent, sometimes they would alter in order of first, second, and third. Hospitality was last every time. Kristen also consistently scored lowest in hospitality. She only scored one point higher than I did, and I always scored zero. We became concerned that we were not welcoming people. Our friends tried to console us and assure us that we were hospitable, but what do they know—they enjoy being around us!

We learned two things about ourselves in this period. First, we are both introverts, and we recover at home. Second, while we enjoy visiting with people in our home, we will both wear ourselves out cleaning to prepare for guests.

Two cats, a dog, and a teenager have cured us from thinking that we have the cleanest house on the block. But the visits with those who serve in different ministry contexts have been our real lessons in Christian hospitality. These visits fill us with such joy that we forget about dust and cobwebs and lose track of time. When we extend the true hospitality of visits with our sisters and brothers in our home, we experience the joy of the Lord's presence.

Hospitality is more than extending a welcome, a place to stay, or a meal to someone. Hospitality is a way to share with fellow Christians and to hear about the work of God in places and lives that may not be a part of our normal pathways. Hospitality expands our world and helps us grow in our knowledge and love of God and neighbor.

DAILY SCRIPTURE READINGS

Genesis 18:1-8	Romans 12:9-21
Matthew 25:31-46	1 Peter 4:1-11
Mark 6:7-12	Hebrews 13:1-6

QUESTIONS FOR REFLECTION

1) Is hospitality difficult or easy for you?

2) How can you think of hospitality as a discipline that helps you grow in your relationship with God?

3) What does it mean for you to do works of mercy like visiting the sick or feeding the hungry as if you were doing them in service to Christ?

4) When have you received Christian hospitality?

5) Learning about what God is doing in different places through those to whom I extend hospitality revitalizes my faith. How have you been encouraged in your faith when extending hospitality to others?

Week Five: Joyful Asceticism

Philippians 3

> "Finally, my brothers and sisters,
> rejoice in the Lord."
> —Philippians 3:1

Today, we rarely use the word *asceticism*. Perhaps we hold bias against the word due to its associations with the most austere spiritual practices of extreme fasting, flagellation, and the wearing of uncomfortable hair shirts. Dallas Willard says when he began teaching about spiritual disciplines in various Protestant churches in the 1970s, most of his hearers shared a common skepticism about asceticism.[1] However, Willard notes, people stayed, heard him out, and seemed interested in what he had to say. I rely on a similar friendly interest to keep you with me at this point. I fear that describing the discipline Paul illustrates in Philippians 3 as asceticism may scare off some readers. You may be thinking, *Now he pulls the big reversal and tries to convince us to practice rigorous disciplines, but he works a little sleight of hand by telling us to do it joyfully.*

I use the word *asceticism* here not to identify extreme spiritual practices but rather in the sense of its Greek root. The Greek verb *askein* means "to practice, to exercise, to work." I mean exercise or practice when I say Paul invites us to engage in joyful asceticism.

My struggle with asceticism stems from prejudices I held against the early church monastics. I thought them guilty of running to the desert to escape temptation. Stories of fights with demons, extended periods of fasting, and all night prayer vigils sounded like spiritual one-upmanship. Yet as I read more about their lives, I understood that they fled to the desert not to escape temptation but to face it. In the sayings collected from many of these early desert monastics, I met people who held a deep sense of humility and forgiveness because of their awareness of their struggles and temptations and a strong sense of the grace they experienced in Christ. Their legends are filled with stories of monastics working out their faith. Abbot Moses, when called to come to judge another brother, enters the assembly dragging a basket of sand behind him. When the others see this display and ask what he is doing, abbot Moses says, "I do not see my own sins running out behind me, yet you call me here to judge another."[2] The desert monastics also offer warnings like that of abbot Antony who recognized that some wear themselves out with abstinence yet grow no closer to God.[3]

These monastics went to the desert to discipline their bodies in devotion to Christ. Admittedly, among them were examples of excess, like the stylites who confined themselves to living on top of pillars and the dendrites who lived in the tops of trees. But the vast majority of these monastics longed to follow Paul's exhortation to train and to discipline their bodies like a finely tuned athlete.[4]

Beware of Boasting in the Flesh

Paul's tone at the beginning of Philippians 3 is very different from Philippians 1. In chapter 1, he says that it does not matter if people preach Christ from impure motives as long as they preach Christ. In chapter 3 he warns against persons he calls dogs, evil workers, and mutilators of the flesh. We do not have enough evidence to identify these opponents. Theories include Jews, Jewish-Christians, Gnostics, and Spiritualists.[5] While we may not easily identify the opponents, we can recognize what Paul finds troubling about their preaching. Paul denounces teaching that places confidence in what we do through our own efforts rather than in God and God's work in us through Christ Jesus. Paul sees this teaching as a denial of Christ and as a strike at the very heart of the gospel, wherein we no longer graciously receive salvation but earn it by our actions. For Paul, salvation is by grace alone. Paul takes issue not with the specific acts he mentions but with boasting in any act as something *we* do to bring ourselves closer to God.

Paul now offers himself as a third illustration of the radical humility for which he calls at the beginning of chapter 2. Paul first catalogs what he could achieve through his works of the flesh. Paul is a model Israelite, born to Hebrew parents, not a convert. He descends from the tribe of Benjamin. Benjamin, the youngest of Jacob's twelve sons, was the only one born in the Promised Land. Saul, Israel's first king, was from the tribe of Benjamin. Benjamin did not side with the northern kingdom in the split that occurred between Israel and Judah under Solomon's son Rehoboam. Paul is heir to a proud Israelite heritage, a Hebrew born

WEEK FIVE: JOYFUL ASCETICISM

of Hebrews. As to his participation in Judaism, Paul says he was a model of keeping the law. He was circumcised on the eighth day, according to the teachings of the Torah. He chose to become a member of the Pharisees, strict observers of the law. He was so zealous in observing the duties and obligations of the law that he felt it necessary to persecute the church. According to such works, Paul says, "I was blameless."

Through knowing Christ, Paul counts what he could gain as loss, his rightful inheritance as rubbish. Paul does not say that the law, the commandments, or Judaism are rubbish. Rather his attempts to earn righteousness before God through such works are trash. Paul tosses aside his confidence in the flesh. He condemns not Judaism but the belief that anyone earns a special place with God through human effort. Knowing Christ has become the most important way to be close to God. Let's be clear: Paul renounces not his *bad* habits but his *best* habits. He is not a former outcast of society who suddenly reformed his manners and discovered the virtuous life.

Today our attempts to place a claim on God may not come through temptations to observe the ritual law of the Old Testament. We face temptation in subtle suggestions that we deserve a privileged place within the church because our parents gave a pew, our grandparents bought a stained-glass window, or the land on which the church rests was the gift of a distant relative. Worse still are the temptations that lead us to think God owes us something and others should take notice of us because we have read the whole Bible, pray fifteen minutes every morning, and give money to help the poor. Such gifts to the church and spiritual practices are not bad, but we succumb to temptation when we place our confidence in them. Paul says place your confidence on the cross.

Losing Our Gains

Through the cross, we forget self and learn Christ. Forgetting self is the power of the resurrection at work in us. Christ's resurrection allows us to let go of our claims and join in the sufferings of Christ; doing so puts behind us our old self. We come to know the power of the resurrection by following Christ in suffering. Paul outlines his model for Christian living. It begins with God's power setting us free in the resurrection of Christ, but the resurrection does not free us from pain and suffering. It calls us to enter suffering as Jesus did in the hope that we will be resurrected with him. Within this framework of the Christian life, Paul gladly renounces everything else to participate in life in Christ. Imitate me in such self-denial, Paul says, rather than in my former actions.

In 1905, theologian Albert Schweitzer took a step that shocked many of his friends and family. Schweitzer had earned PhDs in theology and philosophy. He was well known as an organist and often consulted in the construction of organs. He was a pastor and principal of the Saint Thomas Theological College in Strasbourg. But he wanted to serve in Africa as a missionary. The missionary board in Paris turned him down because of his theology. Schweitzer believed they would not question his theology if he sought to serve as a medical missionary. So, that fall he resigned many of his prestigious posts to enroll as a medical student at the University of Strasbourg. After receiving his medical degree, Schweitzer spent large segments of his life in Africa as a doctor.

I disagree with much of Schweitzer's theology. I think his studies of the life of Jesus and the life of Paul, while helpful, have significant errors. Others charge Schweitzer with being colonial and paternalistic in his medical practice in Africa. But there is one thing I can neither escape nor let go of with Schweitzer: Whatever his faults, his determination to set aside whatever got in the way of his serving the people he felt called to serve inspires me. He is no pristine saint, depicted in stained glass. But as his theological opponent Karl Barth would say, he is one of those unholy people who was claimed by God for God's purposes. What draws me to Schweitzer is not his theological writings or even his medical service but pictures of him serving: The lines on his face reveal signs of deep concern, but a twinkle in his eye suggests his joy of sharing in the sufferings of Christ through the power of the resurrection.

We do not have to travel to foreign lands and serve in another culture to practice the self-denial Paul believes is part of Christian living. Paul's self-denial is even more radical. He wants us to give up our practice of score-keeping when it comes to our religious observances and our subtle beliefs that there are Christians and then there are superior Christians who have done more, know more, or have accomplished more than others. Paul does not recommend that we give up our spiritual disciplines like reading scripture, prayer, fasting, or giving, but that we give up the idea that these practices somehow earn us more credit with God than those who practice them less. Paul calls us to use these disciplines to train our body, mind, and soul to be more aware of God's grace at work in us. We practice spiritual disciplines to gain greater awareness of God, not to master the discipline.

Rather than seeking righteousness that we achieve on our own, Paul invites us to be conformed to Christ, to let the power of Christ at work within us shape our living here and now. Paul is not advocating quietism, that we do nothing, that we simply trust in Christ and that everything will work out OK in the end. Nor does he believe that because we have faith, we can live any way we please. He calls us to press on and not to lose what we have gained in Christ. What we gain in Christ, not what we gain through self, counts in our life of faith. Paul says we should run toward such conformity to Christ.

Eyes on the Prize

I am not sure when I became a runner. For a long time, I resisted calling myself a runner. Other people said I was a runner long before I was comfortable claiming that label. I was running twelve to fifteen miles a week, but I knew I could stop at any point. Even when I started running more than six miles at a time, I told my brother-in-law that the key was getting through the first forty-five minutes. I could give up at any point before that. Once I ran forty-five minutes or so, I figured I was committed. (I was also usually a long way from my house at that point, so the quickest way back was to keep running.)

I still did not consider myself a runner. Real runners got up early and eagerly went out the door to conquer the day's run. I would run for a month or two and then if the rain interrupted my schedule or I was traveling and got out of my routine, I would stop. Months later, I would start again, but I was always frustrated that I had to rebuild my endurance, my leg strength, and, most of all, my commitment. I learned that I have to work toward a goal to stick to my running routine. I now seldom finish a race without my eyes on a future race, so that once I finish one event, I begin training for the next one. This means I do not fall out of practice and lose the benefits of what I have trained my body to accomplish.

Now even I confess that I am a runner. I run in the rain sometimes. I run when the wind seems to blow out of every direction at the same time. This past year I ran on both Thanksgiving Day and Christmas Eve, no small feat for a pastor serving a local church. Don't tell my wife, but I pretty much planned our last two family vacations based on places I wanted to run. When I say I am a runner, I do not mean I am winning any races or setting pace records. I run to discipline my body. I focus on my personal goals in races.

In Philippians 3:12-21, Paul incorporates one of his favorite images for the Christian life: a runner competing in the games. Christ is the prize, the goal, and Paul calls us to follow him in pressing on to this goal of being conformed to Christ. Even his racing toward Christ, Paul points out, is not a matter of his personal effort. Doing so is possible because he has been seized by Christ. Now he seeks to yield himself to this controlling influence until Christ finally transforms his body.

Paul introduces another metaphor for this life at the end of the chapter. He says those seized by Christ now have a citizenship in heaven. Being conformed to Christ looks like living out of our heavenly citizenship. Emperor Augustus made Philippi a Roman colony. Citizens of Philippi had status as Romans citizens. The soil of the city was considered the same as the soil of Rome. While all the members of the church in Philippi may not have been Roman citizens, they would have been aware of the privileges and protections that came with this status. These are the people to whom Paul writes and says, let your life be controlled by the citizenship you have in heaven. Heavenly citizenship is even more important than being a citizen of Rome.

Paul concerns himself with how we use our bodies. He warns that being ruled by the belly and fixated on earthly things places us in danger of losing the prize of Christ. Paul does not say that the body or earthly things are evil. Evil resides in pursuing such things before pursuing Christ. Paul does not call us to a rigorous asceticism that puts our health in jeopardy. He asks us to recognize our temptation to put our hope in pursuing things because of the pleasure they bring our bodies and instead to let our bodies be at the disposal of Christ. Paul begins the chapter with a stern warning against boasting in the flesh. He ends the chapter calling us to train our flesh to be used for Christ and to pursue this goal with all our strength, joyfully pressing forward to the prize of being conformed to Christ.

Some years ago, I took down my "I love me" wall in my study at the church. I had arranged my various degrees and awards behind my desk so that whoever came to meet with me might be as impressed as I am with all my achievements. I learned that the people who came to me for counseling, spiritual guidance, and advice seldom cared about that stuff. They wanted to know if I was willing to listen to their pain, frustrated hopes, and struggles to discern where God is at work in their life. I still have my degrees and awards; they are in my home study if you want to see them. But in my office I now hang pictures, artwork from children in our congregation, and a crucifix. These things remind me to be human, to be a fellow pilgrim on the path of discipleship, and to look for hope in the most unlikely places.

We do not have to sell everything we have, leave our families, and go to the desert like the early monastics to live the asceticism that Paul believes forms the heart of Christian living. Paul asks us to practice an asceticism that confronts whatever would get in the way of us pursuing Christ. Paul does not describe this loss as a painful process that evokes our bemoaning the things we have given up. Paul describes this loss of all things as a joyful pursuit of the loftiest of all goals. We press on toward that goal by joyfully training our body to serve God.

DAILY SCRIPTURE READINGS

Psalm 100	1 Corinthians 9:19-26
Romans 12:1-8	1 Timothy 4:1-10
1 Corinthians 6:12-20	2 Timothy 2:1-7

QUESTIONS FOR REFLECTION

1) What comes to mind when you hear the word *asceticism*?

2) How is the Christian life similar to the training that an athlete undergoes to prepare for competition?

3) Who do you know who has given up something to live out a calling to ministry? What did this person give up and what new skill, training, or ability did he or she have to learn to serve in ministry?

4) What have you renounced so you can live your own calling as a Christian?

5) What tempts you to turn away from your calling so you can indulge yourself?

6) How do you use your body as a living sacrifice to God?

Week Six: Joyful Giving

Philippians 4

> "I rejoice in the Lord greatly that now at last
> you have revived your concern for me."
> —Philippians 4:10

During the financial crisis of 2007–08, I started dreading church meetings. Not that I was ever an enthusiastic meeting attendee, mind you. I am unlikely to say, "Hey, we need more meetings at this church." More and more the meetings I attended were dominated by talks of what we could not accomplish due to lack of funding, ministries that we would have to cut, and news of someone else who had lost a job. We needed to acknowledge these realities, and we certainly needed to be aware of those who were losing jobs. But I began to feel something was missing.

Though I had rarely ever looked forward to meetings, before this time I would leave church meetings with a renewed sense of how being connected to one another in Christ allowed us to achieve more than what we could accomplish on our own. While we supported and prayed for one another in pain and loss, we also celebrated ministries that brought healing, helped people grow in their understanding of God's love, and found new ways to serve others. Nowhere was this uplifting more common than in meetings with other pastors. Even when things might not be going well in the congregation I was serving, I would hear stories celebrating new ministries or new worship services another church had started to reach a new group of people in a given location. I always left these meetings with a stronger awareness that I was a part of something bigger than I often saw in day-to-day ministry. Not only was I encouraged knowing that other pastors and churches were praying for our congregation in times of difficulty, but also I could go back and share in our congregation how God was still at work doing some amazing things in the world. During the financial crisis, I felt our awareness that God was still able to accomplish good things in the world missing from many of our church meetings. I left many of these meetings unprepared to bear confident witness to the joy of the gospel; I felt dispirited.

After attending a meeting of pastors one morning, I found myself sitting in my study, flipping through the pages of an old book. The book had belonged to my father. My father received it from one of his mentors in his first pastorate. It is one of the few books I took from my father's library after his death. I keep the book not just because it reminds me of the connection my father had with his mentor but because of its sheer audacity.

The book, *The Sound of Trumpets*, was published by the Methodist Episcopal Church, South, in 1934 as part of a financial appeal to launch a massive expansion of its missionary work around the globe.[1] Bishop Arthur J. Moore, recently assigned to oversee the foreign mission work of the church, was the main author. Moore describes a great financial need and appeals for generous support of this bold new mission endeavor. He repeatedly appeals to his readers to advance the cause of mission by giving above and beyond what they have been giving to support the ministry of the church.

What strikes me as the audacity of the book is that Bishop Moore outlines this vast expansion of mission through the generous additional giving of Christians amid one of the worst economic situations, the Great Depression. Each time I pick up this book and leaf through its pages again, I am struck by an appeal based on a confident call to expand the witness to the gospel through joyful stewardship, giving, and receiving as a response to what God has already given us. Moore calls the church to the same kind of joyful offering that Paul received from the Philippians.

Giving from Thanksgiving

Philippians is sometimes referred to by scholars as a "Thankless Thanks." It seems obvious that Paul writes this letter in response to a gift of support that the Philippians have sent to help him in his ministry, yet he never comes out and says, "Thanks for the money you gave me." Other scholars have pointed out that Paul opens the letter with a note of thanks; however, his thanks is not directed to the Philippians but to God who is at work in the Philippians.

Gerald Petermen argues that Paul follows ancient letter writing conventions in Philippians, and expressing direct gratitude among intimate friends was unnecessary. Instead, the recipient of a gift often reported on how the gift had been used. Petermen believes that the whole letter expresses

Paul's thanks. After reporting on how he thanks God for what God is doing through the Philippians, Paul turns to a report of how their gift furthered the gospel. He gives them a report on their investment. Their investment is not in Paul but in the gospel.[2]

David Briones believes that Paul has a theological rationale for not expressing thanks directly to the Philippians. Paul understands this relationship not as a direct relationship with the Philippians but as part of a three-way relationship between God, Paul, and the Philippians. God gives the gifts, and the Philippians steward God's resources. For Paul, the type of benevolence he encounters from the Philippians is a fruit of Christian joy. Joy produces generous givers in thanksgiving for what God has done and is doing in the world.[3]

The joy Paul calls us to manifest in our living is not simply optimism or the avoidance of pain and hardship. Philippians 4 opens with Paul's acknowledgment of a dispute in the congregation. He has said already in 1:27–2:18 that one of the most powerful ways the church can witness to the truth of the gospel is by living in unity amid persecution from outside the church and avoiding backbiting and self-seeking within the community. Now he openly recognizes division within the congregation while naming names,

Euodia and Syntyche. It is one thing for the preacher to say, "We should all get along." It is something else entirely for the preacher to say, "I urge Esther and Sally to live together according to the mind we have in Christ," in the midst of a Sunday sermon. (Paul's letter would be read to the congregation during a weekly worship service.)

We know little about Euodia or Syntyche. We do not know if theirs is a personal struggle involving only these two women or if they represent two groups in a division throughout the congregation with everyone taking sides. To Paul, the type of dispute does not matter. If two Christians are disputing, they are destroying the witness of the whole community. So he calls the whole community to live out the joy they have in Christ by remembering what they have received. Joyful giving is born in thanksgiving for what God has already done.

Think on These Things

Paul talks of joy in the Lord. He does not say the Philippians will evidence this joy by walking around with a smile on their face or whistling, "Don't Worry Be Happy." We know joy through expressing gentleness to all, no matter how they treat us. This gentleness stems from confidence that the Lord is near rather than from a lack of concern or timidity. We display joy when we live with confidence in God instead of seeking retaliation when threatened or provoked. Karl Barth says that joy is the great "Nevertheless!" of this letter.[4] Though Paul is in prison, he rejoices. Though the Philippians are persecuted, they should rejoice to suffer for Christ. In the midst of division within the church, the community should come together in joy.

Paul reminds us to do two things when fears and anxiety consume us. First, Paul calls us to pray. For Paul, prayer is more than praise. He calls us to frame our prayers with thanksgiving, and he encourages us to make known our needs to God. Then the peace of God will stand guard over our thoughts. Second, Paul encourages us to meditate on the things that are worthy of praise. Paul believes that by letting our minds dwell on these thoughts, we will turn our lives toward praise. By giving thanks for what God has done and meditating on the excellent things of God, we can frame our requests to God in a way that evokes a joyful desire to share with others from the resources God has entrusted to us.

After I had been a pastor for about five years, I found myself on the verge of leaving full-time ministry. Things did not seem to be going well in the congregation I was serving. In fact, many members were angry with me. My father died.

My wife and I were struggling in our marriage. I started seeing a counselor. After a few weeks of letting me share all the things I thought were going poorly in my life, my counselor asked me to start keeping a journal of the good things that happened each day. I came back a week later with an empty journal. It was my way of saying, "I told you my life is rough right now." The counselor took my journal, looked at the empty pages and asked, "Did you wake up today?"

I said yes. My counselor gave me his pen and said, "Put today's date and write, 'woke up.'" After I did, he congratulated me on making a good start with my journal and went on to ask me about my marriage, my work, and how I was dealing with grief after the loss of my father. We continued seeing each other for several more weeks. Each week, my journal entries got longer. They became less centered on me and more focused on God's goodness. My troubles did not suddenly disappear, but I found it easier to confront them when I assumed an attitude of joyful awareness that God was still at work in the world. My counselor helped me frame my prayers for help in an attitude of thanksgiving while thinking about excellent things.

Joyful Giving and Receiving

Several years ago, I was attending a session of our annual conference of the United Methodist Church in North Georgia. Late in the morning session on the third day, I was weighing the advantages of darting out early to get to a restaurant before crowds started to build or staying until the end of the morning session when more of my friends could join me for lunch. I was leaning heavily toward an early departure (did I tell you I am not much of a meeting guy?) when a man stepped to the microphone. I stayed to listen as he taught me one of the best lessons in Christian stewardship while giving an update on an offering.

Andrus Norak, the president of the United Methodist Seminary in Tallinn, Estonia, reported on the work of the seminary. Our conference had supported the establishment of the seminary. The president told the story of the day one of the students of the seminary came to meet with him. The student had one simple question: "Why? Why would these people from halfway around the world give so generously to support this school and help make it possible for me to be trained and equipped to be a pastor when there is little likelihood that any of them will ever meet me or see the fruits of my work in the ministry? Why would they do this kind act for me?"

Andrus responded, "Because of what Christ did for them."

The student quickly asked another question: "So how can I pay them back?"

"Study hard to be the best pastor you can be and tell other people that Jesus loves them too."

Christian stewardship is born in joyfully receiving, in giving thanks for what God has already done for us. We give not to earn God's benefits or to help God in God's endeavors. We give as a joyful response to what God has done in our lives and as a joyful way to take part in ministries that we may never see or participate in physically but that still bring an awareness of God's love into the minds and hearts of others. Too often, church stewardship campaigns focus on how we need to support the budget or to discipline ourselves to give a little more, to grow in giving more to God and spending less on ourselves. We forget that giving is a joyful way to respond to God's grace at work in us and to join God in work around the world.

Paul celebrates the Philippians' display of this kind of theology and practice of stewardship. Paul begins his acknowledgment of the Philippians' gift by saying he has joyfully received the support they sent through Epaphroditus. As soon as he acknowledges the gift, he launches into a statement about how he has learned to be content in all circumstances. Paul is not embarrassed by their support. Paul wants to be clear that his joy comes not from what he has received but from what their giving means for their growth in Christ. Paul depends not on them and their giving but on God in all situations, whether he has little or plenty. Paul and his needs are not the focus or the reason for the Philippians' giving. They repay a debt, but their debt is not to Paul.

Paul mentions that this time is not the first time that they have sent him support. According to Acts 16–17, upon leaving Philippi after his first visit, Paul goes to Thessalonica to start the church there. In Philippians 4, he thanks them for sending support to help in his work there. Paul even commends them to the Corinthians, reminding the Corinthians how he received help from the Philippians to carry out the ministry in Corinth. (See 2 Corinthians 11:7-9.) The Philippians gave not out of a sense of abundance but in a time of "extreme poverty" (2 Cor. 8:2).

Paul begins to sound like an accountant in Philippians 4:17. He says the profit or interest which accumulates to their account because of their giving, rather than the gift itself, brings him joy. Usually, we do not think of what we give away as helping us gain interest. If I spend money out of my savings account, I typically lose any interest that was building in the six months prior to its withdrawal. Paul is not promoting a prosperity gospel of giving so that God will give us even more. His statement about God supplying the Philippians' needs directs them to be as confident and dependent on God as Paul is. They accrue interest as they participate in the spread of the gospel. By giving to support the ongoing mission work of the church, they not only support Paul but also help take the good news of the gospel to places to which they might never be able to travel and to people they might never meet. They have become investors in the expansion of the kingdom.

In verse 18, Paul shifts his language from finance to the sanctuary. He compares their gift to a fragrant offering that flows up to God. God, not Paul, receives their gift. Paul and the Philippians, through their mutual giving and receiving, act out thanks to God. Thanksgiving manifests through more than words we say with our lips; we manifest thanks to God in how we use the resources God has entrusted to us to participate in God's work in the world.

Greater Works

Marion Edwards was the first bishop under whom I served. He had been elected bishop just before I began to serve my first appointment in rural North Carolina. He came to a gathering of district clergy one day and led us in worship. He preached a sermon entitled "Apportionments." If you are not familiar with this word, *apportionments* refers to the money that each local United Methodist congregation pays to the district, conference, and general church to support the mission and ministry of the worldwide church. Methodists sometimes interpret the word *apportionment* as *taxes* or *franchise fees*, words those in Methodist hierarchy lament as they do not quite capture the theology behind apportionments. In any case, Bishop Edwards preached about the type of giving we often struggle with most in the church: what we give away beyond our local building to people and ministries we may never see in places we may never go.

The bishop preached using John 14:12, where Jesus says that those who believe in him will do even greater works than Jesus did. He began by saying that for years he struggled with this text. Every time he read it or heard it in church, he was reminded that he had never healed anybody, fed thousands, or raised the dead; all things Jesus has done by the time he speaks these words in John 14. But, while serving as a district superintendent, he had traveled from church to church and had shared how each church, through their apportionment giving, was supporting hospitals in Africa and Asia, building new churches in the Philippines and Eastern Europe, and restoring lives through local counseling and rehab centers. Bishop Edwards suddenly realized that through our combined giving to support local and worldwide mission work, we were achieving far more than we often stopped to consider. He shared that he went through a shift from thinking of apportionments as dues that he had to be sure each congregation paid to recognizing them as gifts that connected each local church to the worldwide work of the gospel, something in which each and every person should participate with joy.

Many congregations will ask for a special offering during Lent and designate the funds for a specific ministry: a homeless shelter, a food pantry, and so on. We ask our congregants to participate in special offerings above and beyond their normal giving. When a Lenten offering is about giving more and not about participating more in God's wider work, it may start to feel like another chore to check off the spiritual to-do list. Feeling this way reveals that the focus of this Lenten discipline is too much on us and not enough on the purpose of practicing disciplines. At their best, Lenten offerings help us to participate joyfully in the work of the gospel.

A few years ago, I started focusing less on what I was giving up for Lent and more on what I was adding. I often added by giving up something. For instance, if I gave up chocolate, I not only tried to stop eating chocolate but started estimating what I would have spent on chocolate and setting aside that amount of money to give to a mission that I did not ordinarily support. I did not share with others what I had given up. Instead of always talking about what I was not doing, I talked more about the work I was trying to help support. I was not sad or upset that I was going without something or giving away more money; I was experiencing a joyful Lent through giving to support God's work in the world.

DAILY SCRIPTURE READINGS

Exodus 35:20-29	2 Corinthians 8:1-15
Matthew 6:1-4	2 Corinthians 9
Mark 6:30-44	2 Corinthians 11:7-11

QUESTIONS FOR REFLECTION

1) Does giving feel like a Christian duty or a way for you to participate in God's work?

2) How do you celebrate the ways in which your offerings help further the work of the gospel?

3) How does your church support mission work around the world? How does your congregation celebrate the way financial giving helps support God's work in places that you may not visit or among people you may never meet?

4) Who in your life exemplifies joyous giving?

5) What is the difference between giving as an attempt to earn favors from God and giving as an expression of gratitude for what God has done in your life?

Conclusion: We Call This Friday Good?

As we were leaving the church and heading home after the Good Friday service, my son, Matthew, said, "Dad, I don't get it. Why do we call this day *Good* Friday? This is the day when we remember the death of Jesus on the cross. What is so good about that?"

My son was asking the same question I had asked my parents years before. Countless Christians ask the question year after year. What is so good about Jesus' death on the cross?

When I was in high school, I found a tape of a sermon by Tony Campolo. In the sermon, Campolo tells about a Good Friday sermon he heard that captures the paradox of the cross for Christians. The preacher on that Good Friday worked one phrase over and over again to speak to the reality of Christ's suffering and the hope of Christians. The phrase was, "It's Friday, but Sunday is coming!"[1] As

Christians, we always see the cross through Easter. Yet we cannot fully appreciate Easter if we do not acknowledge the pain and death of Good Friday.

Paul places this tension about the cross at the heart of Philippians by inserting it into the hymn in 2:6-11. Paul looks at the cross through the lens of Easter and Easter through the lens of the cross. By placing the cross in the center of the hymn, he places the cross at the center of his argument and in the center of Christian living. He uses the cross as a call for Christians to confront and engage suffering. He reinforces the centrality of the cross in Christian life when he refers to those who oppose the faith as "enemies of the cross" in 3:18.

In raising the crucified Jesus, God overcomes suffering and death. The cross then becomes the ultimate sign of victory and a source of joy in Christian living. We can now accept hardship with joy because we know that Christ already has confronted the worst, and God did not abandon him. Thus, the cross serves as a Christian sign of joy in any circumstance.

The cross keeps Christian talk about joy from slipping into wishful thinking or denial of reality. Paul speaks of joyfully practicing his Christian life from a jail cell. His joy is not based on his situation or the goodwill of his friends.

Through the cross, Paul finds a joy that allows him to live in the midst of pain and suffering with joy.

The paradox of Good Friday lives in the irony that we cannot develop a Christian theology of joy without the cross and that the theology of the cross—an instrument of death—points to joy. In *Laughter: A Theological Reflection*, Karl-Josef Kuschel says Christian joy is not an optimism that ignores difficulty. Christian joy has the cross behind it. "It is joy with a garland of mourning."[2]

Throughout Philippians, Paul speaks of practicing disciplines like prayer, hospitality, and giving not to gain joy but as joyful expressions of the life we now live in Christ. In Philippians 3:10-11, he outlines the power of the resurrection as leading us through suffering to resurrection. Christ's resurrection is not the end of all suffering but the power at work within us to endure suffering. Spiritual disciplines are expressions of this resurrection power at work within us. They give us the strength to say with Paul, "Because of this I rejoice," no matter our circumstances.

May the joy that finds expression through such disciplines as prayer, witness, humility, hospitality, asceticism, and giving continue through all the seasons and direct all your living to the glory of God.

LEADER'S GUIDE

This Guide is designed to help facilitate small-group sessions during the season of Lent. The role of facilitator can rotate through the group or remain with one person throughout the series. The plan is for a six-week study that focuses on one chapter each week. The introduction can be combined with the first week and the conclusion with the last week. For one-hour sessions, a group of eight to twelve participants is ideal; groups larger than twelve might consider dividing into smaller groups or allotting more than one hour for meeting.

The group can gather in chairs placed in a circle or around tables where all participants can face one another. Participants may find it helpful to keep a journal as they read to record thoughts, questions, and ideas that occur from the chapters as well as insights from the daily scripture readings and responses to the questions at the end of each chapter. Encourage participants to bring a copy of the book, a Bible, and their journal each week.

At the beginning of each session, the facilitator should remind participants that no one is expected to respond to every question. Each participant should feel free to participate verbally at times and to participate through listening at others. It is common for groups to experience increased participation as the sessions progress. The facilitator will need to be attentive to when the group needs to linger longer in one area and when the group needs help to move forward.

Session Format

Gather (3-5 minutes): Allow participants to greet one another and find their seats. Remind members that verbal sharing is not required, and the decision of those who choose not to speak should be respected.

Opening Prayer (1-2 minutes): This prayer can be a brief extemporaneous invocation of the Spirit's presence or a short printed prayer that the group might say together.

Scripture Reading (5 minutes): Ask someone to read the week's passage from Philippians. Before the reading, let participants know that a minute or two of silence will follow the reading so that everyone can listen to and reflect upon the text in silence.

Responding to the Text (20 minutes): Ask participants to share what they heard from the text either from the reading they just heard or from their own reading and study during the week.

Adopting the Discipline (20 minutes): Speak the word for the discipline connected to the week's chapter: *Prayer*, *Witness*, *Humility*, *Hospitality*, *Asceticism*, or *Giving*. Ask participants to share what they have learned about this discipline and how they practice it or now have resolved to practice it.

Praying for One Another (10 minutes): Invite members to share joys or concerns that they would like to lift up in prayer. Close in prayer. This prayer could be a group prayer led by one individual, or members could pair up and pray for each other. Experiment with different ways to pray together as a group throughout the sessions.

NOTES

Introduction: Laughing on Ash Wednesday

1. Gregory L. Bloomquist, "Subverted by Joy: Suffering and Joy in Paul's Letter to the Philippians," *Interpretation* 61, no. 3 (2007): 270–82.

Week One: Joyful Prayer

1. Karl Barth, *The Epistle to the Philippians* (Louisville: Westminister John Knox Press, 2002), 10.
2. Fred B. Craddock, *Philippians*, Interpretation: A Bible Commentary for Teaching and Preaching (Atlanta: John Knox Press, 1985), 17.
3. World Council of Churches, "In God's Hands: The Ecumenical Prayer Cycle," https://www.oikoumene.org/en/resources/prayer-cycle.
4. Harvey Cox, *The Feast of Fools: A Theological Essay on Festivity and Fantasy* (New York: Harper&Row, 1969), 147–49.
5. Richard J. Foster, *Celebration of Discipline: The Path to Spiritual Growth* (New York: Harper Collins, 1988), 2.
6. There are many different prayer books with daily scripture readings and prayers available. Both the Book of Common Prayer and the *Celtic Daily Prayer* have daily offices that are accessible online: http://www.bcponline.org/DailyOffice/dailyoff.

html and https://www.northumbriacommunity.org/offices/
how-to-use-daily-office/.

Week Two: Joyful Witness

1. Two books that have helped me learn how to share my faith are H. Eddie Fox and George E. Morris, *Faith-Sharing: Dynamic Christian Witnessing by Invitation* (Nashville: Discipleship Resources, 2003) and James R. Adams, *So You Can't Stand Evangelism?: A Thinking Person's Guide to Church Growth* (Cambridge, MA: Cowley Publications, 1994).
2. Robert Jewett, "Conflicting Movements in the Early Church as Reflected in Philippians," *Novum Testamentum* 12, no. 4 (1970): 362–90.
3. Martin Luther King, Jr., *Why We Can't Wait* (New York: Penguin Books, 1964).
4. King, 71.
5. King, 84, 91.

Week Three: Joyful Humility

1. Brother Lawrence of the Resurrection, *The Practice of the Presence of God*, trans. John J. Delaney (New York: Doubleday, 1977).
2. H. A. Williams, *The Joy of God* (Springfield, IL: Templegate Publishers, 1979), 102.
3. James O'Mahony, "Joy in Praise" *Orate Fratres* 2, no. 3 (1928): 78.
4. The word translated "conceit" in verse 3 is *kenodoxia*. This word can be translated literally as a "vain glory." This is opposed to the type of living Paul prays the Philippians will live in 1:11, a glory to God. (Ralph P. Martin, *Philippians* [Grand Rapids: William B. Eerdmans Publishing Co., 1991], 89.)

5. Karl Barth, *The Epistle to the Philippians* (Louisville: Westminster John Knox Press, 2002), 57.

Week Four: Joyful Hospitality

1. Lucian of Samosata, "The Passing of Peregrinus," trans. A. M. Harmon (Cambridge, MA: Harvard University Press, 1936), par. 12, http://www.tertullian.org/rpearse/lucian/peregrinus.htm.
2. Donald Wayne Riddle, "Early Christian Hospitality: A Factor in the Gospel Transmission," *Journal of Biblical Literature* 52, no. 2 (1938): 141–54.
3. See *Didache* 11 and 12 (http://www.newadvent.org/fathers/0714. htm); the phrase, "Fish and visitors stink in three days" is attributed to Ben Franklin in *Poor Richard's Almanac* (Waterloo, IA: The U.S.C. Publishing Co., 1914), 21.
4. Paul's use of the word *son* is itself an expression of Christian hospitality. Paul uses the intimate term *teknon* (child) instead of *uios* (son) to emphasize "the intimate personal relationship between the two men." (Peter T. Obrien, *The Epistle to the Philippians* [Grand Rapids: William B. Eerdmans Publishing Co., 1991], 325.)
5. Martin's vision of Christ is told in his biography by Sulpitus Severus, chapter 3, available online at: http://www.users.csbsju. edu/~eknuth/npnf2-11/sulpitiu/lifeofst.html#tp.
6. John Wesley, "On Visiting the Sick" *Wesley Center Online* (Wesley Center for Applied Theology, 1999), http://wesley.nnu. edu/john-wesley/the-sermons-of-john-wesley-1872-edition/ sermon-98-on-visiting-the-sick/.

Week Five: Joyful Asceticism

1. Dallas Willard, *The Spirit of the Disciplines: Understanding How God Changes Lives* (New York: HarperSanFrancisco, 1988), 19. Chapter 8 includes a history of asceticism in the Western Church.

2. Helen Waddell, trans., *The Desert Fathers* (New York: Vintage Spiritual Classics, 1998), 101–2.
3. Waddell, 103.
4. Waddell, 13. In the introduction to her translation, Waddell describes the early monastics as "athletes of God."
5. Jewett, 362–90.

Week Six: Joyful Giving

1. Arthur J. Moore, *The Sound of Trumpets* (Nashville: General Commission on Benevolences, Methodist Episcopal Church, South, 1934).
2. Gerald W. Peterman, "'Thankless Thanks': The Epistolary Social Convention in Philippians 4:10-20," *Tyndale Bulletin* 42, no. 2 (1991): 261–70.
3. David Briones, "Paul's Intentional 'Thankless Thanks' in Philippians 4.10-20." *Journal for the Study of the New Testament* 34, no. 1 (2011): 47–69.
4. Barth, 120.

Conclusion: We Call This Friday Good?

1. Tony Campolo uses this story in multiple talks and sermons. You can find videos of his telling of it on YouTube by typing, "Tony Campolo It's Friday" in the search bar. He has also written a book by this title in which he features the story of the sermon. *It's Friday but Sunday's Comin'* (Nashville: Thomas Nelson, 1984).
2. Karl-Josef Kuschel, *Laughter: A Theological Reflection* (London: SCM Press, 1994), 84.

FURTHER RESOURCES

Commentaries on Philippians

Barth, Karl. *The Epistle to the Philippians: 40th Anniversary Edition.* Louisville: Westminster John Knox Press, 2002.

Beare, F. W. *A Commentary on the Epistle to the Philippians.* New York: Harper & Row Publishers, 1959.

Cousar, Charles B. *Philippians and Philemon.* Louisville: Westminster John Knox Press, 2009.

Craddock, Fred. B. *Philippians.* Atlanta: John Knox Press, 1985.

Martin, Ralph. P. *Philippians.* Grand Rapids: William B. Eerdmans Publishing Co., 1976.

O'Brien, Peter T. *The Epistle to the Philippians.* Grand Rapids: William B. Eerdmans Publishing Co., 1991.

Osiek, Carolyn. *Philippians Philemon.* Nashville: Abingdon Press, 2000.

Vincent, M. R. *Critical and Exegetical Commentary on the Epistles to the Philippians and to Philemon.* Edinburgh: T&T Clark, 1897.

Books on Spiritual Disciplines

Foster, Richard J. *Celebration of Discipline: The Path to Spiritual Growth, Revised Edition.* New York: HarperSanFrancisco, 1988.

McLaren, Brian. *Finding Our Way Again: The Return of the Ancient Practices.* Nashville: Thomas Nelson, 2008.

Willard, Dallas. *The Spirit of the Disciplines: Understanding How God Changes Lives.* New York: HarperSanFrancisco, 1988.

Books on the Theology of Joy

Cox, Harvey. *The Feast of Fools: A Theological Essay on Festivity and Fantasy.* New York: Harper Colophon Books, 1969.

Kuschel, Karl-Josef. *Laughter: A Theological Reflection.* London: SCM Press, 1994.

Moltmann, Jurgen. *Theology & Joy.* London: SCM Press, 1973.

Morrice, William. *Joy in the New Testament.* Grand Rapids: William B. Eerdmans Publishing Co., 1984.

Williams, H. A. *The Joy of God.* Springfield: Templegate Publishers, 1979.

CPSIA information can be obtained
at www.ICGtesting.com
Printed in the USA
BVHW040712060219
539470BV00011B/107/P

9 780835 817936